51 SALES TIPS
KEYS TO SELL MORE
AND SUCCEED SELLING
(Salesman's Thoughts 2)

Title: 51 Sales Tips, Keys to Sell More and Succeed Selling

Series: Salesman's Thoughts

Series Volume: 2

Author: Raúl Sánchez Gilo

All rights reserved

© Copyright 2018 Raúl Sánchez Gilo

Cover: Rosamaría Bertol Astasio

First Edition: 2018

ISBN-13: 978-1723203589

ISBN-10: 1723203580

51 SALES TIPS

KEYS TO SELL MORE AND SUCCEED SELLING

(Salesman's Thoughts 2)

Raúl Sánchez Gilo

*To all those who have supported me,
and especially to Rosamari, Betty and Lima.*

INDEX

PROLOGUE _____ 13

CHAPTER 1: ON SELLING _____ 19

Tip nº 1. Ten Sales Tips that weren't Sales Tips _____ 19

Tip nº 2. The Way of Excellence to Succeed Selling _____ 21

Tip nº 3. The Trust in Sales _____ 27

Tip nº 4. The Client is still the King _____ 31

Tip nº 5. The Art and Science of Selling _____ 32

Tip nº 6. The Importance of Knowing the Needs of your Clients ___ 34

Tip nº 7. The "Secret" of Selling without Selling _____ 36

CHAPTER 2: ON SALESPEOPLE _____ 39

Tip nº 8. Logos, Pathos and Ethos _____ 39

Tip nº 9. Some Mistakes of the Salespeople _____ 41

Tip nº 10. Essential Skills of the Salespeople _____ 44

Tip nº 11. The New Seller's Perspective _____ 46

CHAPTER 3: ON LISTENING AND ASKING _____ 49

Tip nº 12. Listen to your Client _____ 49

Tip nº 13. The Active Listening _____ 50

Tip nº 14. Smart Questions _____ 54

Tip nº 15. On Types of Questions _____ 56

Tip nº 16. Try it, Ask your Clients _____ 58

Tip nº 17. Try it, Ask your Clients (II) _____ 60

Tip nº 18. Do not Argue with your Clients _____ 62

Tip nº 19. The Non-verbal Communication _____ 64

CHAPTER 4: ON THE COMPETITORS _____ 69

Tip nº 20. Avoid Competing only for Price _____ 69

Tip nº 21. Keys to Differentiate from the Competition _____ 71

Tip nº 22. Keys to Differentiate from the Competition (II) _____ 76

Tip nº 23. Competitive Benefits and Advantages _____ 80

Tip nº 24. Customer Service as a Competitive Advantage _____ 84

CHAPTER 5: ON THE PRICE _____ 89

Tip nº 25. How to Sell More without Lowering the Price _____ 89

Tip nº 26. The Price Objection _____ 93

Tip nº 27. The Best Strategy to Price Objection _____ 95

Tip nº 28. Tips and Ideas for Overcoming Price Objections (I) _____ 98

Tip nº 29. Tips and Ideas for Overcoming Price Objections (II) _____ 107

Tip nº 30. Beyond the Price (I) _____ 113

Tip nº 31. Beyond the Price (II) _____ 115

Tip nº 32. Beyond the Price (III) _____ 119

Tip nº 33. Beyond the Price (IV) _____ 122

CHAPTER 6: ABOUT THE CUSTOMER EXPERIENCE _____ 127

Tip nº 34. About the Customer Experience _____ 127

Tip nº 35. The Customer Experience (II) - the Perceived Value _____ 130

Tip nº 36. The Customer Experience (III) - the Influence on the Brand _____ 132

Tip nº 37. The Customer Experience (IV) - The Loyalty _____ 134

Tip nº 38. Customer Experience Tools _____ 136

Tip nº 39. The Prospect Experience _____ 138

CHAPTER 7: ON PROSPECTING _____ 145

Tip nº 40. Generating New Opportunities - Prospecting _____ 145

Tip nº 41. Searching for Potential Clients _____ 150

Tip nº 42. Importance of Opportunity and Prospect Qualification _____ 154

Tip nº 43. Prospect Qualification – BANT Method _____ 155

Tip nº 44. Beyond BANT _____ 163

Tip nº 45. Initial Keys in the particular case of RFQ/RFP _____ 168

CHAPTER 8: ON THE SALES PROCESS _____ 173

Tip nº 46. The Sales Process _____ 173

Tip nº 47. The Previous Preparation _____ 178

Tip nº 48. Development of the Proposal _____ 180

Tip nº 49. On the Objections _____ 185

Tip nº 50. Keys to Remember in Any Negotiation _____ 188

Tip nº 51. Considerations on the Closing _____ 192

CHAPTER 9: THE VISIT OF CR _____ 199

Author's Note _____ 203

PROLOGUE

Thank you very much for purchasing this book. These 51 Sales Tips are sure to inspire and motivate you in your profession. But you don't just have to read them. You have to make them your own and act accordingly. Only then you will be able to sell more and succeed selling. Some will be more useful to you than others for your particular case. Some will change the way you think about selling. But everyone will help you to fulfill your dreams and personal goals.

In this regard, I like to think that these lists of tips are like commercial pills, small doses of medicine to improve the disease of bad sales. As such, they should be taken continuously and repeated as often as necessary. Of course, without choking.

Second book of the Salesman's Thoughts series

This is the second book of the "Salesman's Thoughts" series, a series of ideas, concepts and thoughts that will help you sell and understand the fundamental and timeless concepts to succeed in your profession, whether you are a professional salesperson or a sales manager, a CEO, an entrepreneur or you have a relationship with the entrepreneurial and business world. At the end, we're all salespeople.

It is necessary to clarify that it is not a series in the style of fiction sagas where the plot remains unfinished from one book to another, but that they are independent books, although they complement each other and share several common concepts.

Some advice insists on concepts discussed in the first book of the series, as it could not be otherwise ("Sell More and Better, Eternal Sales Techniques beyond Internet", which I will cite from here on as "Smab" to shorten), ideas that, due to lack of space, needed to be expanded and nuanced.

It also includes, with modifications and further explanation, some of my most popular publications and articles in social networks and blogs, which seek by this means a greater exposure and permanence than the temporary one they had in their day.

Many other sales tips, most of them, are unpublished, trying with all of them to deal with a great variety of issues and sales topics of great application in the current and future business world. In any case, all of them respond to the same sales philosophy, which is the one I want to share.

Stop fighting and your client will thank you

I don't believe in ready-made recipes for selling, nor in the need to learn phrases, question types, models of answers and counter-answers, nor in the many so-called sales tricks that have become so widespread in many manuals on the subject. In these practices, what prevailed was the seller's interest in selling at all costs, based on predefined conversational traps, where the client/seller duality was considered as that of a battle, as a game of hunting or fishing where the prey was the client.

In every battle there are winners and losers; winning a battle does not mean winning the war, and doing an operation does not mean winning a client. Old practices may be useful in some cases, but nowadays they are not enough. Stop fighting and your client will thank you...

You can learn to sell with tricks, but you will always find new situations for which there is no script, unless you understand how to sell more through the real balance between products, sellers and customers, the one that looks to the long term and is not only based on optimizing customer satisfaction, but also aims to obtain and strengthen their loyalty.

The current paradigm has completely changed. The main focus is on the client and in our relationship with them, a relationship that is based on trust and above all on providing value, on giving to receive. The client is the king, we've given them all the power and they don't want to lose it.

In line with the above, this book of sales tips aims to provide that necessary additional value and to offer the salesperson, the entrepreneur and anyone else involved in the business world, a series of concepts, ideas, experiences, inspiration, motivation and also own beliefs, which will help them to be more successful in their profession, in their company and with their business. Beliefs that are the result of my years of experience as a salesman, and that have led me to discover what works and what does not.

My personal experience

I have visited over 30 countries, and have sold high-tech products in over 60, including the organization and delivery of multiple seminars, conferences, presentations, customer and distributor trainings, sales meetings, countless trade shows, etc.

As a director and sales coordinator I have been involved in B2B industrial sales, as well as in B2C sales. I have been a distributor and have been on the other side of the table, helping distributors grow in their market. I have opened new markets, new countries, looking for representatives, evaluating them, training them and giving them all the necessary support and assistance to maximize sales in each area.

This necessarily involved maintaining and improving the business relationship with these distributors and customers, keeping a constant search for new ways to grow together in the market and also developing a close cooperation, which leads to getting to know the people behind the jobs, to understand their motivations, their day-to-day problems, and ultimately, to always look for the best way to meet both the needs of representatives and their end clients.

The variety of cultures, customs, ways of doing business, as well as the multitude of people you meet and learn from, lead you to seek common values that can be applicable to all situations, to understand the hidden truths behind each experience, positive or negative, and to learn from mistakes and successes.

In this search, these beliefs have become values, not absolute truths, but they have proven their effectiveness in the world of sales, and will continue to do so, as many of them are eternal, universal concepts that will always be applicable to any field, any industry and at any level.

Then you contrast those values with the trends and concepts in vogue that the experts and sales gurus advocate, and you realize that behind the fashions and high-sounding names that pretend to be novelties in the world of sales, there are always a series of sales techniques and eternal concepts that we should not forget, and that are the necessary basis for not only improving our commercial understanding but also that of human nature. It is also necessary to highlight the importance of having a concrete sales process, not only to sell more, but also to improve it by being able to analyze where and why we have not been successful. That is precisely why the last two chapters are dedicated to important stages of this process.

Objective of the book

Even if you find in this book just one valuable advice for you, I will have fulfilled my objective, which is to help all the professionals involved in the commercial, business and sales world to be more successful in their jobs. I am not only referring from a labour perspective but also from a personal one, because many of the advice are related with the part of humanity that we are somehow losing lately with the rise of new and multiple technologies. In today's complex business and sales world, we must vindicate the human side of selling and the social aspect that sales have always had.

Precisely, it is this client/salesperson duality that must be broken. We are human, persons, and that is what we must not forget when selling. However, we must not go crazy and forget the business part either. It is not a matter of forgetting to sell, but of selling differently and more effectively.

Therefore, although one may think that many of the tips in the book refer to the B2B environment, most of them are also applicable to B2C, where this paradigm shift is also taking place. Brands today do not want to win customers, but to conquer their hearts, and in the midst of all this noise, excess information and advertising bombing, the competitive difference is made by people and ultimately the sales based on trust and human relations.

I have not classified the tips under any strict logic, although they are listed by similar topics that I have grouped in chapters. It is not necessary to follow an obligatory reading order, it is also possible to jump from one to the other, but it is advisable the indicated by the index.

On the other hand, I wanted to start each tip with one or more quotes by great wise men, some classical and others modern, who continue to inspire us, encourage us to reflect on them and enrich each advice itself. I hope, reader, that you also find them interesting.

Each of the tips on the list can be, and indeed are, objects in themselves of many other books, and in that sense I hope they also serve to motivate the curious reader to delve deeper into any of them.

I have tried to make them brief, and thus be able to complete the list of 51 in a reasonable number of pages, easy to read and understand. It is not a step-by-step guide, nor does it pretend to be a sales bible, since there is no such thing that responds to everything, neither of this nor of any other matter.

Go ahead, reader, start the medication, each tip is a pill that will help you sell more and succeed selling. You don't need a medical prescription, just the motivation to improve yourself and grow professionally and personally, which is what it's about as well.

CHAPTER 1: ON SELLING

Tip nº 1. Ten Sales Tips that weren't Sales Tips

"The best way to find yourself is to lose yourself in the service of others." (Mahatma Gandhi)

Serendipity is discovering something valuable and unexpected accidentally, discovering it when you are looking for something different, a lucky find. Interestingly, the word has its origin in a traditional Persian tale called "The Three Princes of Serendip", in which the protagonists, princes from Serendip Island, the ancient Persian name of present-day Sri Lanka, solved their problems through coincidences.

Without being a prince, this serendipity found me that day in the following way:

I was waiting for someone in an old school which no longer worked as such for many years. I was thinking about my things, including this book, and looking for a place to sit when casually, or causally, I saw an old sign on the wall that caught my eye. It was probably there for decades, and possibly it will be many more, as the site did not seem like it would be reformed shortly. But it had stood the passage of time, and even though it wasn't so bright anymore, it still held a kind of magical light that encouraged such serendipity. Its title was "The Welcome Decalogue", a list of advice written by a deceased former local bishop, supposedly to better welcome any visitors, people in need, relatives, etc., and that once illuminated the minds of the students with the following tips:

The Welcome Decalogue

1. Each person is a gift, here, now and always.
2. To facilitate the meeting is to get it right.
3. To welcome is to start well.
4. Smile is the best therapy.
5. Listen to the end is the best welcome.
6. I make your needs my own.
7. Everything human interests me.
8. Eye contact is our friendly lifestyle.
9. Welcome to the house of my heart.
10. Thanks for coming, thanks for being here.

Casually, or causally, it seems like a modern list of tips from any customer service and support expert, or keys to improving the much-named customer experience. Reread each of the tips from that perspective, substitute person by customer and you tell me whether they are wise and appropriate sales tips or not.

They are very appropriate for any salesperson, especially when attending or receiving a client's visit. Sure they are not all that should be, but I'm sure all of them are.

In fact, it refers to several of the timeless principles that will appear in this book and that are necessary to keep in mind to be successful selling, among others, such as: understanding the customer's needs, not forgetting the human and personal side, the importance of listening to sell, addressing the customer's heart, the key of the sincerity and trust in sales, making easy and pleasant the customer experience from the beginning, connecting with the customers and thanking them for choosing us.

The old is the new, and the new is the old ... Welcome your customers. This is your serendipity of today, and it's not a tale. Always remember this Decalogue and welcome your customers. They are the most important part of your business.

Tip nº 2. The Way of Excellence to Succeed Selling

"We are what we repeatedly do. Excellence, then, is not an act, but a habit." (Aristotle)

There are many features and skills that are required of the salesperson, but apart from these, there are certain routines that are obvious but essential to being a successful seller, regardless of the product and the company. Therefore, it is important that we list them, understand them and make them our own:

- **Wanting to help clients**: we must ask ourselves at all times what is the best way to help our customers and ask them too. This genuine attitude of wanting to help will be one of the biggest drivers of the seller's success. This attitude will be recognized and rewarded by the clients, as it will generate the necessary trust to commit to the salesperson and to become loyal customers to the brand, product or service (see also tip nº 7, the Secret of Selling without Selling).

- **Sell value, value and more value**: we must never stop selling value, we will never tire of repeating it. We must always go beyond price and discounts. Regarding them, do not rely on a possible final discount to close a deal. In that way we mislead clients, accustoming them to that routine that does not add value but reduces it (see chapter 3, On the Price).

- **Generate new opportunities**: the salesperson should never forget to prospect and create new opportunities, do not get stuck in the existing ones. For this, it is important to set aside working time for this task, and not to stop doing it even if it does not produce immediate results. The opportunities must be generated, not just expected. This means that a large part of the daily or weekly plan must be aimed at prospecting, looking for new clients and projects (see chapter 4, On Prospecting). Don't forget that one of the best ways to find them is to ask current customers, especially to satisfied customers, who can give us references for other potential customers.

- **Wanting to create relationships**: we buy from people we like, whom we get on well, whom we have some understanding, have good relationship, respect and trust. It's all about creating a good and genuine relationship with the customer, having that attitude, following it and getting it. If you get the customer's trust, you get the customer. And the competition will not be able to do anything against this (see also tip nº 3, the Trust in Sales). The excellent salesperson mainly seeks to create that relationship with his clients, who in turn will bring other clients, recommended by those clients thanks to the relationship and building of trust.

- **Follow a long-term plan**: any plan, even a bad one, is better than no plan at all. We need to establish a way forward, a plan for day-to-day activities. You can deviate from it by the daily events, urgencies and unexpected issues that arise, but always with the awareness of returning to the established plan as soon as possible and knowing at all times what the planned process is. This means having a day-to-day control, and knowing when you have not fulfilled the plan and what actions you should take to follow through in the following days. But targets aren't just daily targets. It is important to comply with them, we have said that it is essential to be consistent and have a day-to-day plan, but we must not lose the long-term perspective, the monthly and/or annual objectives, which makes these goals more attainable and also reduces pressure and anxiety. You must keep in mind that there are and there will be bad days, ups and downs, but the optimism we mention below, together with an awareness of long-term objectives, will allow us to overcome all the obstacles. The salesperson must have vision and perspective of the future, and in that sense he should start from his annual target and not only look at the results of a week, knowing that it is more important the constancy and results maintained throughout a longer period of time than the ups and downs of the day to day (see also chapter 8, On the Sales Process).

- **Constancy**: constancy, constancy, constancy, I will not tire of repeating it either. The objectives are not met in a day or two, it's a long-distance race. It takes discipline. There is no need to stop, there is no need to keep celebrating your day-to-day successes, nor regretting your failures. Whatever happens, good or bad, don't stop and what matters is constant effort, perseverance and keep working, which is also closely related to the previous point of always having a plan to follow.

- **Prioritize**: we must focus on the hottest opportunities, where closing is most likely. There are customers who are still studying your solution, they are not ready yet to make a decision and it is not convenient to force it, although we must not lose sight of them and should be followed, but we must always prioritize the opportunities that are closer to their resolution. On the other hand, some clients take more time, others less, but you should not miss one because someone else calls or because distractions or emergencies arise. Don't leave things half done, nor the client. Each client should feel like he is the only client, regardless of whether the seller later assigns priorities in private, but always, always, everyone should feel heard and valued (see chapter 7, On Prospecting).

- **Approach**: related to the above and also to the famous Pareto principle, it is necessary to focus our efforts on what gives us the best results, to look for that 20% of causes or actions that produce 80% of our results. In short, to select where and how we target, which customers have more potential and which are not worth losing a lot of time. This does not mean that we do not attend all clients, but we do have to stablish priorities and focus our work on the real objectives (see tip nº 42, the Importance of Opportunity and Prospect Qualification).

- **Optimism**: this is not only a necessary attitude for the seller himself, but also for the client, who sees and feels it; it is reflected in the relationship with them and mainly in the complaints or claims that are also opportunities and not just problems. Complaints are great opportunities to build customer loyalty through our good service. The ability to solve problems requires this optimism and positivism in order to finding the right solutions (see also tip n° 24, Customer Service as a Competitive Advantage). Optimism is also essential in everyday life, to overcome daily refusals and obstacles, optimism that is one of the keys to success. An optimistic salesperson sells more. Much better if he is also a happy seller, since this is reflected in the client and he will convey that optimism and happiness that our clients also need and seek.

- **Learning from mistakes**: sometimes you win, sometimes you lose, but you always learn. This means that by learning from these mistakes we try not to repeat them again. But you have to be humble and recognize them, and at the same time to have vision to detect them, because many times they are mistakes that we are not informed about, or the clients do not tell us about them, unless we ask them, and therefore it is also essential to seek excellence by searching for and preventing the mistakes that can occur. This is also closely related to the analysis of which actions give us the most results and which do not, to monitor our work and adjust those ineffective jobs, optimize processes and make as few mistakes as posible (see also tip n° 46, The Sales Process).

- **Disconnect**: it is not productive to work to exhaustion, in fact it is counterproductive. It is necessary to rest, disconnect when necessary from work, relax, have our time and get enough sleep. All this will increase our productivity.

- **Always look at our product or business from the customer's point of view**: why do we sell differently than how we buy? Put yourself in the customer's shoes, and think how they like to buy. Look at your business and your product from the eyes of your customer, put yourself in their place, have empathy and really understand what they need (see also tip n°6, the Importance of Knowing the Needs of your Clients).

- **Training**: the excellent salesperson must be constantly in training mode. The market and your customers so require it. You must have a routine and concern for learning, for continually improving the way you help your clients, for being an expert in your field and for being curious not only about your market but also about everything around you, a genuine desire to know and grow as a person and as a professional (see also chapter 9: The Visit of CR)

- **Competitiveness**: which is related with the desire to improve and grow from the previous point as well as with the optimism necessary to be better than the competition, with the also mentioned constancy and with the ability to fight daily, self-confidence and proactivity. The excellent salesperson enjoys competing, has fun selling, and this is reflected in his or her daily routine (see also chapter 4: On Competition)

In short, our actions define who we are. If we want to be excellent salespeople we have to repeat many of these habits until we excel in them.

Excellence is not easy. Nothing worthwhile is. In the case of salespeople and sales such excellence can only be achieved by repeating good habits, by determination and perseverance in doing better every day and not forgetting these key tips to achieve your sales goals. Practice, repeat and repeat until they become habits.

Tip nº 3. The Trust in Sales

"A wise person does not teach by words, but by his actions."
(Lao-Tse)

As mentioned, there are concepts that never change in the world of sales, and one of them is the importance of generating and achieving the trust from the customer.

In fact, nowadays the brands are extremely concerned about gaining the trust of the latest generations of customers, both the so-called millennials and the next generations, who are precisely unbelievers of these brands. They have a multitude of options to choose from and the way to avoid getting lost among so many offers is mainly the references they get from their friends, contacts, social networks, etc. In short, from the word of mouth from their closest friends, rather than from the efforts those companies can make to achieve this credibility and trust. Although the means and the ways change, it is necessary to recover these principles in the commercial activities and in the relationship with our clients.

In this regard, I would like to tell a personal story related to trust and respect. It has to do with the sales lessons that a tiny screw can give us:

It was many years ago and probably it wasn't exactly like this, but that's how I remember it. We were trying through a new distributor to enter the difficult Japanese market, to sell them electronic equipment (yes, it sounds pretty bold...). It took us nine months to get into that market and start selling.

During the process the representative required a demo equipment and we shipped one to them. A few days later they returned the unit to the factory. They found a tiny screw was missing from the base. Probably unscrewed in transport. It wasn't functional; they could have used the unit without any problem. They could have replaced the screw by themselves. But they returned the equipment and paid the transport cost.

We might have thought that they were not our ideal distributors, too fussy ... But we didn't complain. We placed the screw and shipped back the unit.

Other stories came up, but we finally entered the market. The lesson of the tiny screw was related to those concepts that are so fashionable today: trust and respect.

Nowadays, it is said that you must first earn the trust and respect of your potential client before they becomes your client. That's what it was. The Japanese knew that centuries ago. Maybe that's why one of the characters in my first book is Japanese, among other things.

It wasn't really a question of quality; they didn't doubt the quality of the company or the product. They had clear, as something normal and accepted in the industry, that demo units are not new units and can have scratches but they work perfectly, which is what is needed for a demo. It's like asking for a second-hand car to be like a new one. They were clear that the new units complied with all the required quality standards and that was not the problem.

The key was to build trust and mutual respect as the basis of the relationship, and that required going through, let's say, some "tests" to know each other, build trust and ultimately recognize each other as partners. After all, you don't marry the girlfriend the day you meet her, it has a process. The same goes for the clients.

Therefore, we must always keep in mind that business relations are based on trust. And such trust is perfected through our actions, rather than through our words.

Trust and respect may be common to all cultures, but in each one they follow or develop through different ways that need to be explored, as in the case of the story we have told.

In that sense, with each client we must have the attitude to listen and adapt to their circumstances, their beliefs, respect their decisions and their way of buying. Each client has different characteristics that we must respect and we cannot act in the same way with everyone. We must combine this with our ability to show ourselves as expert sellers and leaders in the sector. This will be a key factor in building their confidence and deepening their loyalty.

The salesperson generates confidence in the customer when he is really interested in helping them, when he is looking for a super service, not selling a super product. The seller must want to provide excellent service (see also tip no. 24), to be an advisor for the client, a consultant, an expert who solve their problems, not who create more problems to them. Attitude is very important for building trust, so the client should notice that you work to help them, not to help yourself.

This also includes not exaggerating or lying about the benefits of our products and services, being honest, ethical and honest with the customer, not talking bad about competitors or other customers, maintaining a consistent pricing policy and without discrepancies between similar customers, not trying to sell what the customer does not need and not hiding problems that may arise, but solving them.

Trust is not built only after the customer has bought, but it must be encouraged long before the potential customer becomes a qualified prospect (see also tip n° 39, the Prospect Experience), even before we have them as target. All the latest tools for social selling, content marketing, education and maturing of leads and prospects, brand and product image creation, etc., which are ultimately nothing more than means of increasing the customer confidence in our option, must contribute greatly to this.

Similarly, in the prospecting process, the potential customer should think that the seller understand their problems before they can trust the possible solutions.

To that effect, reducing the psychological costs and associated insecurities perceived by the customer regarding our product is also a key factor in increasing their confidence in our offer (see tip n° 32).

Thus, the best salespeople build trust throughout the entire process. But one of the essential ones is also at the moment of fulfilling what has been promised. Fulfill what was sold, with the value announced, with our commitments. And make sure that we meet the expectations created, which we do not have to increase inappropriately. We have to generate realistic expectations that will produce the necessary confidence.

In short, trust is one of the elements of the eternal equation for success in selling, one of those that will never go out of fashion; it remains more current than ever and permeates most of the advice in this book.

Customers don't buy from people they don't trust. Do I need to tell you more…?

Tip n° 4. The Client is still the King

"The great knowledge begets big doubts." (Aristotle)

The information age has changed the rules of the game and the way customers buy. The customer is the one in control. It is clear that the company and the seller must adapt to their needs. Starting from the client to the solution, and not the other way around. The client is still the king; we've given them all the power... And they don't want to miss it!

In this Internet age, before talking to any salesperson, potential buyers have already greatly advanced their purchase and knowledge of your product, viewing your website and the one of your competitors, looking at social networks, blogs, comparing opinions, etc. Customers go through more than half the process on their own. So when clients contact a salesperson, they need to be provided with something else than everything they have already researched in their advanced purchasing process.

The seller will have to adapt to this great change and to these new technologies and above all will have to specialize to be able to provide that additional value that the client needs.

He will be a professional salesperson, or he will not be seller.

But beyond the latest technological changes, we are human beings and that will not change. We will continue to need to analyze the customer's needs, get to know them better, discover their desires and motivations, sell added values, define our value proposition, know and differentiate ourselves from the competitors, improve the customer experience, seek their satisfaction, convert each sale into the beginning of the next with a proper sales process, satisfy their needs and build customer loyalty.

You might not see the forest for the trees. The seller is still more necessary than ever, showing the right way to the client as an expert, as a guide and consultant in their industrial sector, niche or market. It is the duty of the seller to integrate his knowledge in his product and market with his knowledge of the client and his needs, adapting his value proposal to each client to help him buy.

The client is the king, but like every king, they need someone to advise them...

Tip nº 5. The Art and Science of Selling

"A painter is a man who paints what he sells; an artist, on the other hand, is a man who sells what he paints" (Pablo Picasso)

Is selling an art or a science? There are many opinions about it. I recently read this sentence: "sales are 80% science, 20% art, and the art is knowing when to apply science", with which I do not entirely agree. The percentage will vary with each situation and with each person. The art is to create value, and in sales you cannot forget the human side and the emotional part derived from human interactions.

Art moves people, and it has always been about generating emotions, giving meaning and reaching the heart. In that sense, we seek the same thing with the art of selling, motivating, moving, transmitting, reaching the heart of the customer and ultimately moving him to buy. Art make us fall in love and we want to make the customer fall in love as well, we want to get their commitment and loyalty to our brand or product.

But sales is also a science, with its laws, rules, methods and measurable data, especially with the multitude of tools for business data analysis, markets research, customer relationship management systems, the multiple branches that study and analyze consumer behavior, neuromarketing and neuro-sales, multiple methods and formulations of sales processes together with marketing analysis, social selling, online and offline sales process automatisms, not forgetting everything related to psychology, persuasion techniques, etc.

We talk about knowledge, knowledge of sales techniques, sales processes and strategies, of knowing the product, the market, the salespeople and above all the clients. Of course, the whole sales process has a part of science.

While, and although we can apply certain formulas to sales, they will always have the relational, human component, which gives them flexibility and the results are not guaranteed as a result of an equation, which is always subjective.

Each person is a world and there are no foolproof recipes to sell in all cases and to all people, so creativity is necessary with each client, it is a game of empathy and relationships. And all this applied to sales turns it into art. There are not two equal customers. Sales are fueled by science, and results are materialized with relational art.

The good salesperson must provide value, humanity, honesty and skills along with all the necessary sciences to not only close the sale but to get loyal customers. In the end it must be a balance between science and art with a creative approach. The secret of success lies in the balance.

For this, one of the sales tips that must keep in mind the salesperson, a sales manager or the owner of a company, is to be continuously learning and updating about new technologies and the advances that science can provide to their profession. But without forgetting that science should not replace art, but complement it.

Tip n° 6. The Importance of Knowing the Needs of your Clients

"Happiness is a balance between reason and desire." (Aristotle)

This tip, with some modifications, was also part of Smab, but I think it is necessary to insist on the great importance it has and therefore it could not be missing in this series of sales tips.

In this regard, you can hear many times: "we must create the need for the client..." I will not tire of repeating it, needs are not created, man has always had the same specific or natural needs, they are universal, innate to the human being and they are not created. It is the way to satisfy such needs, creating and building new means for it, the ones which changes throughout history and societies.

We could say, metaphorically, that needs are like the second law of thermodynamics, the one that says: "energy is not created or destroyed, just transformed." Similarly, the ways of satisfying the same needs change, in the same way that today a car is used when in the past it was used a horse carriage.

Needs are not created, but they need to be stimulated and motivated. You have to know and recognize those needs, find out which one is behind each client and study how to meet them.

In order to define all the actions addressed to satisfy the customer, we can use the classic classification of the needs of Maslow's hierarchical pyramid. While there are many other models and interpretations, this is the most widespread and is sufficient from the point of view of the seller and its objectives. This pyramid included the following needs: physiological, security, social, self-esteem and recognition, spiritual and self-realization.

The curious reader can go deeper by himself and search the Internet for a more detailed explanation of each of the mentioned needs.

The common denominator to all of them is the search for happiness. We all seek happiness, although it is usually elusive. We wait for it without previous appointment. We want it, even without knowing it. We miss it, dream it and imagine it.

What are the main ingredients of happiness? It's a daring list. As always, not everyone will agree, but let's try to think that they were for example: peace, health, love... and you choose the last one. And your clients also choose it. For some it will be money, which they say it doesn't provide happiness. For others it will be work, family, for others pleasure, success, social relationships, maintaining the illusion or even just living in the present... some seek it within themselves and others everywhere.

Regarding the point of living in the present and place barriers to happiness, sometimes our fears of the future and frustrations of the past are the ones that prevent us from being happy in the present, and are also the same fears and frustrations that often prevent your customer to buy. In this sense, rather than looking for what motivates the clients, sometimes the point is looking also for what discourages them, whose roots are often in the past and in the future, in the fear of not making mistakes or not making the same mistakes again.

Put yourself in the shoes of your clients, and try to find out what makes them happy. Try to discover their motivations and desires, their past and future fears, what are the ingredients they seek on their way to happiness, what are their needs according to the mentioned scale, and above all, how can you help them?

In this sense, selling is to satisfy the needs of the client, one of the basic principles, but not the only one...

Tip nº 7. The "Secret" of Selling without Selling

"I slept and dreamt that life was joy. I awoke and saw that life was service. I acted and behold, service was joy." (R. Tagore)

There is much talk about selling without selling, which seems a contradiction, although it is not. It is a phrase that can be found in hundreds of articles, sales trainings, conferences, books, etc.

But it's not just that you don't look like you sell when you sell, it's about the sale happening spontaneously as a result of solving the client's problems.

It is related to being authentic, genuine, being interested in others and awakening that necessary trust in the client who perceives that you are not trying to sell them, but to help them.

Selling is not the ultimate goal, but helping to buy. The most successful salesperson is one who has a passion to serve, engage and add value. He/she doesn't force the sale.

But at the same time that seller tries to be better, different, more effective, faster and more consistent than their competitors.

That salesperson thinks from the client's perspective, understands their motivations and tries to meet their needs.

He/she wants satisfied clients, not just to sell more products, and tries to advise, share knowledge and service. Add value, save time and effort for the client, is the goal.

All the above generates trust and respect. And the sale simply happens naturally as a result.

Another classic sentence that is often repeated in this regard is: "people love to buy, but hate to be sold to", which is related to what we said. The customer does not want to feel the pressure of the seller. He will buy when he is ready to buy, when he's got the necessary trust, not when the seller wants. The customer is the one who decides.

Of course, the seller must defend his value proposal, but always seeking to satisfy the customer, and not for the sale itself. It is about convincing and persuading, not about manipulating or imposing.

We speak about trust, about client's motivations and desires, feelings and emotions, about values beyond the price. In short, it's about human relations.

It is not about selling with the head but with and from the heart.

The "secret" of selling without selling is not in the process, nor in the appearance, but in ourselves...

It is said that all great changes begin with oneself. We must first look in the mirror and understand why the client does not want to be sold to. He wants to make the decision for himself, and then, if he trusts you, if you have previously given him value, then he will look for you, and buy you.

Don't sell, help to buy. That's selling without selling.

CHAPTER 2: ON SALESPEOPLE

Tip nº 8. Logos, Pathos and Ethos

"If you wish to persuade me, you must think my thoughts, feel my feelings, and speak my words" (Cicero)

For those who saw it on Smab and for those who didn't, it's a pleasure to review again these important skills of any salesperson, which in turn are also sales tips:

It is said that by selling you have to convince, but not only that. To sell is also to persuade. We said that convincing moves reason, while persuading instead moves feeling and will. Persuasion has to do with emotions and sensations, while convincing is more related with logic and the head.

Electricity requires two opposing poles to work. Likewise, selling needs to connect the rational with the emotional, the data with the ideas.

We should also remember the classics, because we keep thinking about what Aristotle said in his "Rhetoric". I am referring to the three pillars of Aristotelian rhetoric that define the art of persuasion: Logos, Pathos and Ethos. The Logos has to do with reason and the head, with the speech based on knowledge, logic and empirical facts. Pathos would have to do with the emotions and feelings in the message that can change the mood of the listener or the client in our case. The triangle is completed by the Ethos, with the necessary authority and credibility provided by the seller and his ability to generate trust in the customer, his prestige, charisma and reputation. Convince, Persuade and generate Trust.

Precisely today, customers and consumers are surrounded by multiple data and bombarded with information (logos), they lack the necessary trust in brands (ethos), and therefore it becomes increasingly necessary to appeal to emotion to persuade them (pathos). In any case, in the world of sales it is necessary to combine all of them.

On the other hand, we should not confuse convincing with informing, which is often a mistake of many salespeople who become walking brochures. It is always required an additional argumentation that includes benefits and differential advantages with respect to the simple enumeration of characteristics of a product or service. It is also essential that the conclusions of this argumentation be supported by facts, evidence, verifiable and credible data. For the same reason, we must not go too far and confuse convincing with imposing an opinion.

Similarly, persuasion should not be confused with manipulation or deception, since our objective is always to win the customer loyalty and that they repeat the purchase, to get their commitment and not just to sell them a product sporadically.

Persuading has more impact than convincing, but if we only persuade, sooner or later, the client reflects and concludes that he has been deceived, and that our proposal does not convince him. In that sense, you have to combine both, convince with arguments and persuade with emotions.

A clear example should be a commercial engineer. The part of engineering is the one that must convince, and the commercial part is the one that must persuade. As mentioned, for both purposes is very important the credibility and ability of the seller to be perceived by the client as an expert in their field, with a personal branding image that generates trust in the client regarding his argument.

And you? Ask yourself, are you just simply trying to convince?

Tip nº 9. Some Mistakes of the Salespeople

"Knowing yourself is the beginning of all wisdom." (Aristotle)
"We have other men's vices before our eyes, and our own behind our backs." (Seneca)

To sell, it's necessary to know your product, your company and your customer. But it is also essential to know yourself as a salesperson, because you are also part of the product.

We must start by knowing ourselves, by knowing human reactions and emotions, our own and those of others. In that sense, selling is quite related with empathy, with putting yourself in the other person's shoes.

Knowing ourselves includes recognizing our mistakes. We must make an exercise of introspection and assume the need to improve ourselves.

I hope that the following list, with some of the main mistakes to avoid, will make the curious reader think about his own, recognize some of them and motivate him to overcome them.

Of course, the list is not exhaustive, there are many more, as many as sellers, as many as people and situations, but if at least you avoid the following, you will greatly increase sales:

- Not knowing the client properly.
- Lack of deep knowledge of the product and the company.
- Not making good use of the material and sales tools.
- Not listening and talking too much.
- Having arguments with the client.
- Not using emotions to motivate buying desires.
- Not knowing how to defend the price.
- Not knowing how to counteract purchase objections.
- Closing the sale weakly or not closing it in time.
- Lack of constancy and working capacity.
- Not using differentiating elements.
- Focusing too much on the product and not on the client.
- Not filtering properly the potential customers and pursue pointless opportunities.
- Not knowing the essential sales techniques.

Many times it is our eagerness to sell what makes us make such mistakes. We don't focus on the client, on helping them, on trying to discover their needs, we improvise on the fly and we don't look for ways to solve their problems. This leads us to exaggerate, to lie, to be unclear, to not provoke a desire to buy because we don't know the customer, we don't listen to them, we talk too much, we give "masterly" speeches, the price becomes the main topic of discussion, we don't close, and all this is combined with the lack of constancy and knowledge of sales techniques (which should not be confused with "sales tricks").

We are afraid of the "no" and not selling, but instead we are not afraid of not helping, when that should be the main objective. Fear of losing the sale, but on the way we lose the client... we hear, but we don't know how to listen, and if we don't ask and listen, we cannot know their needs.

If we don't know or try to know our client we become sellers without soul, who will not offer solutions, just products, and of those there are thousands and most of them similar, undifferentiated. But the differential advantage can be the seller himself, the one who is really interested in knowing his client and provides him an additional value.

Another great error, prior to those on the mentioned list, is the lack of a plan, of prior planning. Before any meeting with a client it is necessary to have it minimally prepared (see tip n° 47) and to face it with a lot of information and previous work. You have to do your homework. Likewise, it is very important to know our product in depth and become experts on it. Knowing the product also means knowing your company, the characteristics of your market, and your customer accordingly.

We must also remember that one of the keys to success is creativity. We are in the era of innovation, and so the excellent salesperson must be creative, look for new ways to satisfy the customers, apply creativity to differentiate, find new ways to help them and new solutions to build their loyalty.

Work on improving yourself. Do you make any of these mistakes when you sell? Look at yourself in the mirror. Right now.

Tip nº 10. Essential Skills of the Salespeople

"The most difficult thing in life is to know yourself" (Thales of Miletus)

Salespeople are required to have many characteristics and skills. Some are more specific and many are common to other professions as well. In fact, and among many others, the ability to listen, to empathize and to generate trust can also be demanded of a doctor, a lawyer or an architect, for example.

But the salesperson must develop them even more to become an excellent salesperson and succeed selling.

Selling has always been a social thing, and as such it depends on people. The influence of people on sales results remains superior to processes and technology. In some lower-level commercial positions and some of the simpler B2C situations it may be true that a good, structured and well-defined sales process can correct the possible limitations of the seller and even be immune to the rotation of such salesperson.

But in more complex sales, especially in B2B environments, the weight of the salesperson and their skills has a greater influence on the final success. Even with a good process, which is a necessary but not sufficient condition, it is necessary that good salespeople can get the optimal performance of this process with the capacity and development of their personal skills.

For this, the good salesperson must mix attitude with aptitude and be in constant learning. It's not something magical, but training is needed and keep improving and polishing these skills.

Many are obvious, they have been repeated thousands of times, but as they are often not met and are essential, it is good to remember them:

- To know the product and the company in depth.
- To have a thorough knowledge of the competition.
- Get to know the client in depth.
- To practice active listening.
- Know how to ask smart questions.
- Know how to sell features+benefits+advantages.
- Know how to differentiate from competitors.
- To have a sincere desire and attitude to help the customer to buy.
- To have empathy and the ability to put oneself in the client's shoes.
- To be creative.
- To have perspective and vision of future.
- To have self-motivation.
- Enjoy their work and have passion.
- To have a constant desire to learn.
- To be able to generate trust and credibility.
- To be constant.

Knowing well what we sell, our market and our customers, putting ourselves in their shoes with empathy, gives the client security and confidence, and us the credibility of being professionals, especially if we sell benefits and advantages that differentiate us from the competition, with the firm and genuine intention of helping the customer to buy, meeting their needs in the most creative way possible, and always trying to improve our solutions to build customer loyalty with a perspective of future.

This includes practicing active listening which must be combined with the ability to ask intelligent questions, along with the motivation and willingness to learn constantly, all of which are the result of passion and the ability to enjoy selling (see chapter 3: on Listening and Asking).

There is a lot of talk about selling has changed and that customers have changed as well. Both statements are true, but that does not mean that we forget practical and universal principles, such as the ones on the list. Let's not go crazy with just new technologies, new practices and tools or sales techniques that promise to transform the commercial reality or that explain everything just from the cortex.

All the skills and abilities listed above are a real added value for sales professionals and are of course appreciated and valued by customers. Let's not forget them.

Tip nº 11. The New Seller's Perspective

"The only thing that doesn't change is change itself."
(Heraclitus)

One of the essential skills of the excellent salesperson is his perspective and vision of the future, which allows him to see what others do not see, adapting to market changes and even anticipating those changes.

Well, one of those changes that the seller has to anticipate is that of reinventing his own commercial profession. It has been said and repeated that the Internet has completely changed the relationship between clients and vendors or companies. Apart from the online purchase, we have said that much of the purchase process is done before contacting a seller. It affects not only B2C but also B2B. The client has searched, studied, compared and advanced in their search for solutions before contacting a company or going to a store. The client knows almost everything about your product and company before they meet you. And you, on the other hand, don't know them yet... You're at a disadvantage.

In this sense, the salesperson must be able to provide an additional value that the customer has not previously found in the company's website, in that of your competitors, in their searches for opinions, articles, blogs, etc. The salesperson must become a consultant and help the customer in their buying process, helping through the consultative sale to make the best decision.

They must also provide excellent service, enhance the customer experience beyond the virtual through personal relationship and highlight their value proposition regarding to the current and future problems of the customer. Either that or their future will be to be replaced by robots, by artificial intelligence, if their work doesn't go beyond being an order taker or a customer dispatcher.

But don't worry so much, new technologies won't completely replace the salesperson. Of course, there will be certain jobs that will disappear. Those in which there is no additional value added. But new ones will also be created.

All the digital transformation will affect new patterns of purchase and consumption and many sociocultural changes that will produce new and multiple opportunities for growth. There will be new sales channels to which the professional salesperson will have to adapt. But there will always be a relational component, a balance between human and artificial intelligence.

Despite so many changes they say the future will bring, many of the skills of salespeople most appreciated by buyers will remain the same: trust, kindness, professionalism, patience, presence, empathy, sincerity, honesty, integrity, creativity, flexibility, responsiveness, communication, management, and acting always to benefit the interest of the client. Some things never change.

As we said at the beginning, today's companies are not looking to win customers, but to win their hearts. And that cannot be done by a robot. A machine has no soul or beliefs, technology will never have the spirit. Selling is human and between people, and that means talking about emotions, both those of the seller and the customer, that must be considered and combined, and many times they are the ones that will decide the sale for one side or the other.

Change your perspective. Don't become a robot.

CHAPTER 3: ON LISTENING AND ASKING

Tip nº 12. Listen to your Client

"We have two ears and one mouth so that we can listen twice as much as we speak." (Epictetus)

The salesperson must not only know how to speak, and be able to convince and persuade, but first must be able to listen. Listening is the basis of the sale. In fact, the one who has to talk is the client, who needs someone to listen to him.

You don't have to talk for the sake of talking, nor give great masterly speeches. The salesperson must not make a monologue, but must let the client speak and encourage an open conversation.

Don't waste time boring the customer with a prefabricated and repetitive speech and not really focused on what the customer needs. Listening will save time and effort for us and the client (see also tips no. 30 to 33).

If you listen you show that you are interested in their problem, that you put yourself in their place, with empathy, and that you have a real interest in meeting their needs.

The client offers us information and information is power. Without such information we cannot identify the real opportunities for our proposal.

Now, talking about satisfying their needs and finding previously the problem, sometimes what the client thinks and expresses that needs is not really what he needs (!) It is necessary to find out why he needs it and look for the real problem behind it.

Let's give an example: I may have leaks in some pipes and I may think that I need to repair those leaks, which I think are due to the bad joint of those pipes. But really the problem can be because the pressure pump provides too high pressure, which is damaging the whole circuit and causing these leaks in the joints. I really need a pressure reducing valve at the beginning of the installation to prevent it from happening any more. In the first case the seller may be able to fix an apparent problem, but not the real one. In the second one we go beyond what the client says he needs, which is not always what he really needs, we go straight to why. This change of attitude when looking for the problem will really lead us to find the right solution which is not necessarily what the customer thinks it is.

But it all starts with listening. If we do not listen, and have not previously found the problem, we cannot provide solutions.

Listen, listen a lot, and you'll sell more.

Tip nº 13. The Active Listening

"In order to know how to speak it is precise to know how to listen." (Plutarch)

We have said that a good salesperson should be an expert in his market, but also that he never stops learning. That's why those who really excel listen and absorb any additional information that their clients provide about their niche or market. Listening is also a learning opportunity, and turning the client's message into new value propositions, an opportunity for personal and professional growth.

For this, it is necessary to put into practice a series of attitudes such as being empathetic (which does not mean that you have to be obligatorily sympathetic, but it ends up being a consequence), being positive, having a genuine desire to help the client, being curious and always willing to learn new things, having an open mind, enjoying the conversation, and being sociable in general.

All this is also really part of what we call active listening, which differs from other less complete ones in which we listen without really paying attention.

So, other possible tips to improve active listening with customers are:

- **Take notes of what your client is talking about**: it is common in meetings, it shows interest and helps you to organize the key points to make your own argument, as well as not forgetting any that are important. In any case, it is essential to take mental notes, to summarize, to retain the most important points and to order these ideas in our minds.

- **Do not interrupt the client's speech**: it is not a matter of listening to refute, our intention is to understand them. Interrupting conveys the feeling that we are not interested in what they tell us. That doesn't mean we shouldn't ask questions to better understand what they want to tell us if necessary, either to clarify or to confirm part of the message.

- **Don't prejudge**: preconceived judgments about any issue or about the people you are dealing with lead you to not listen and to not being able to find out what we need to help the other person.

- **Avoid distractions**: in the past it was not necessary to say it, but today it is becoming necessary to remember that we must avoid technological distractions that even become a lack of respect for the customer. If we are looking at the phone continuously we do not listen and if we answer calls while we are in a meeting the communication is unnecessarily interrupted. The mobile phone, better off, in silent or set apart. And the same applies to any other device. It is necessary to concentrate on the present meeting.

- **Trying to connect**: you don't necessarily have to agree with the customer's point of view, but as we are interested in understanding them, the customer's opinion is more important than yours. Your point of view does not give you new information to work with. Of course, it is also important to look for common points to increase our capacity to connect with the client, and if possible, to connect emotionally. People continue to buy from people, and especially from those with whom they connect and share interests.

- **Listen to what they don't say**: we must not only listen to what customers say, but also to what they don't say, and ask ourselves why they don't say it, which will also be related with our knowledge of the customer, with their current circumstances, their company, their type of job and position and their attitude towards the seller. We must try to go beyond words and look for the cause of what we are hearing.

- **Smile**: don't forget to have good humor although this does not mean you have to be funny. In that sense, we must not forget something very necessary and human: please smile. I repeat: smile. Your client's mirror neurons will appreciate it.

While we are mainly referring to the case of the customer/seller relationship and the various points of contact of both throughout the sales process, we must not forget that we must also listen to our customers through other means, such as listening to what they say through their social networks, forums, publications, on their websites and blogs and their opinions and product reviews. In general, to listen to them wherever their voice helps us to better know and understand their problems, motivations, current and future projects, and if possible, what our customers think about our products and those of our competitors.

By the way, listening should be a constant throughout the whole process, not just until the contract is signed ... Before, during and after the sale you have to keep listening. To such an extent that asking questions and listening to the customer after the purchase will be the basis on which to build their satisfaction and possible loyalty to the product or service. Listen to their complaints, problems, reviews and suggestions with your product or service and learn from them.

One of the key points in this process is the complaint management. On the other hand, complaints are free information about mistakes that will help us improve. We need to know these errors to avoid repeating them, and they are options not only to recover a client but also to build customer loyalty if such after-sales service has been excellent, increasing also the possibility of giving us positive references with other customers.

One of the best opinions we can have of a client is "I have felt heard" or "they have understood me". When people feel heard, they feel valued. It's about empathic listening, putting ourselves in the client's place, understanding and accepting them. It's not about pretending that we listen while we think what we are going to say with prefabricated or prepared answers. We listen to help. A type of listening that generates trust, which we have already said is essential for selling today.

Therefore, are you willing to really listen or do you prefer to continue talking too much? The ball is in your court...

Tip n° 14. Smart Questions

"You ask me why I buy rice and flowers? I buy rice to live and I buy flowers to have something to live for." (Confucius)

We have said that it is very important to listen to the client, but ... in order for the client to speak, you must also ask. But not just any questions, but questions addressed and above all quality questions. And it's not about conducting interrogations....

Selling should not become an annoying interrogation for the client and we must not make them feel uncomfortable. Instead, you should have a healthy conversation skillfully directed with your questions. And beyond solving problems, we must also seek to be partners of the client, in line with their present and future objectives.

The best salespeople ask their customers and prospects many quality questions to fully determine their needs, problems, desires and expectations. Ask the right questions and the potential customer will tell you what they want and how they want it.

We must always seek to ask intelligent questions, those with whose answers we can work, seek valuable information to know and understand their business, problems and their relationship with their current suppliers, their business expectations, current projects, what they expect from our proposal, etc.

But the most important thing is that these answers we want to obtain must be specific, measurable and realistic, with clear objectives and within a time frame. This is especially relevant when qualifying prospects (see tip no. 44, Beyond BANT).

Only in this way we will be able to adapt our solution to their real problems and needs and be able to really highlight the benefits and advantages that can really be valued and accepted by the client as such (and not wrongly focus on those that will not be valued).

In many cases this proposal will have to be personalized, making more relevant the need to ask targeted questions to get answers that allow us to help them.

In short, ask smart questions to obtain valuable information. Quality questions to sell more.

Ask questions, listen, understand and add value.

Tip nº 15. On Types of Questions

Judge a man by his questions rather than by his answers."
(Voltaire)

We've said we should ask smart questions, but what kind of questions?

Let us first remember what has been said many times about the seller having to start by asking open questions and then refine them with closed questions (yes or no) or with alternative questions (between two options).

Open questions are essential to begin to know the client's needs. We try to know: who, what, where, how, when, which and why. With them we show interest in the customer and help us to conduct the dialogue. Closed or alternative questions are not usually used at first and make sense when trying to reach an agreement, close the sale, or confirm data, needs, problems, or any other issues that require such confirmation during the open questions phase, and also to narrow down options at the closing phase.

All this is fine, but in practice the problem arises when the client's answers are too general, broad, unclear and even ambiguous. The salesperson is usually left with the idea that the customer has responded, but the information they give us does not help us in practice, it does not help us to help them.

For example, as an answer to one of our open questions, we can accept that of a client who says yes, that this year they plan to invest in new equipment or machinery for their company. Generally, the seller takes this information for granted and, eager to sell, immediately tries to offer them his equipment or machinery. But that information is not measurable, nor specific, nor does it have a deadline. We are interested in knowing why, how, when and what objectives they have. We are interested in knowing, for example, if they plan to invest in new machinery because they want to expand the factory, and for example, if they want to enter a new market; if they are developing new products for their customers, what problems or competition they have in said new market or product, what challenges they have, what is the budget allocated to each package of the project and what specific deadlines are being considered; we are interested in knowing the problems that they may have in the process to comply with all this and how we can help them to achieve these objectives within the deadlines and with the solutions and options that are best adapted to their plans in a realistic way.

Knowing all this information we can have data on which to base a more convincing proposal and in which to add value, since it will be more in line with their needs. For the same reason, we will have more and better arguments beyond the price and the price war with the competition.

In short, before moving on to more closed questions, it is necessary to get answers to the open questions that be, as we have said, more specific, quantifiable, realistic and within a defined timeframe or plan. All this while keeping an eye on what the competition can offer and analyzing what options the client has on the table or may come to have and what advantages and benefits they are looking for mainly.

There can be thousands of examples, as well as questions adapted to each case, situation and client. In fact, the curious reader may find lists and series of typical questions on the Internet, but the important thing is to understand the concept in order to adapt it to the particular market, product or service of the seller.

In other words, to offer more solutions than just products, we must first find out the problems, contrast their problems with our solutions, and focus on the advantages and differential elements that do meet those needs, which will produce the greatest perceived value.

We can also mention as a reference the classic and famous SPIN method where through 4 phases of questions prior to the introduction of your product in the conversation (Situation, Problem, Implication and Need-payoff questions), the clients are led to discover their problem first, make them explicit, that they want to solve it and understand the negative impacts of that situation, to then propose our product, our solution to their problem.

The curious reader may deepen more about it, but the important thing is to understand that this and any other similar method focuses on getting the customer's attention in finding solutions to their problems and that they discover, with more or less enthusiasm, the series of advantages and benefits of achieving it with your product, while building a personal relationship of trust.

Now ... Do you already know what to ask?

Tip nº 16. Try it, Ask your Clients

"Everything we hear is an opinion, not a fact. Everything we see is a perspective, not the truth." (Marcus Aurelius)

We don't just have to ask our customers at the time of selling. It is just as important to ask them later, to find out if they are satisfied or not and to know if there has been any problem. The goal is not to sell something and then disappear.

It should be remembered here that only a small percentage of customers complain effectively. Specifically, more than 95% of dissatisfied customers are silent and do not let you know. Most simply leave, do not buy again and we are not aware about it.

Another of the points to improve our strategy is to encourage the client to express their opinion; for that, they must not think that it is useless, they shouldn't have any difficulty in doing so (without cumbersome procedures) and it should not involve a confrontation. The customer must have the constancy and security that the company is concerned about the satisfaction of its customers and there must be clear and defined communication channels between the client and the company.

If you don't have a defined service, department or system for solving customer complaints or claims, it is time to think about the benefits of retaining a customer (getting a new customer is much more expensive than retaining an old one), and understand that it is not just an after-sales service, but part of the loyalty plan and sales strategy.

But that refers to the reactive part, and for the curious reader there are many books and information on the Internet on how to better integrate these services (for example using the CRM) and how to optimize them. But what I want to emphasize in this tip is the proactive part, not the reactive one. Do not wait for customers to complain, let's not wait for them to ask us, let's ask them first.

On the other hand, asking the customer helps to build a good service experience, improves our relationship with them, increases their confidence through the attention we give them and can reinforce their loyalty and recommendations to third parties.

Do a very simple test, pick up the phone, and call for example a dozen of your clients, even those you think are good ones, and ask them:

- What would you like to change about our service?
- What needs have we not met?
- What would be ideal for you?

Try it. The answers will surprise you...

Tip nº 17. Try it, Ask your Clients (II)

"The man who asks a question is a fool for a minute, the man who does not ask is a fool for life." (Confucius)

We are all obsessed with how to sell more, and how to sell better to customers. The thing is, sometimes we complicate our lives too much. We think so much about ourselves that we don't think about them, about our customers.

We have said that the focus should be on the customer, and start from the client to the solution and not the other way around. Actually, the answer to this how to sell more is a why... Why do they buy from us?

Do the exercise of thinking why your customers buy from you. Take some time and be honest with yourself. Think mainly about what is your most important value proposal for them.

Now try again, call for example a dozen of the last customers who bought from you and ask them:

- Why did they buy from you?
- Why wouldn't they have bought you?
- Why would they buy from the competition?

Contrast their answers with the ones you thought they were.

If they are the same, congratulations!

If they're not, then you have the answer to how to sell more. It depends on knowing what your customer values most about your product or service and what they would not like to see changed.

You can rethink your value proposition based on these answers, analyze how you convey it, if it really is the one that reaches the client and what is the real perceived value of your offer.

It is also very important to analyse the reasons why they would buy from the competition. These answers will give you clues to strengthen your customer loyalty strategy, to know what should not fail to make them go to the competition and what are the future threats that you must prevent to avoid losing customers.

On the other hand, it can also be a great exercise to understand if the clients experience is being pleasant, to know what they value most about it and if there are barriers that can hinder that experience.

Try it. You might be surprised.

Tip n° 18. Do not Argue with your Clients

"A long-lasting argument is a maze in which the truth is always lost" (Seneca)
"Not necessary to turn off the light on the other, to get ours shine" (M. Gandhi)

To have an argument does not lead anywhere. Or just to lose the sale.

You can hold opposing positions, but never have an argument. At any case, each one in its place, without feeling intimidated. Nor should we fall into servility or promise what cannot be fulfilled. Nor, on the contrary, in the passivity and indifference.

At the other hand, if what the client expects or wants cannot be supplied, there is no point in arguing.

You're not going to win an argument, because we both lose, us and the client. And we all have difficult days. What you have to do first of all is just listening. Sometimes it's their fault. Sometimes it's ours, but it doesn't really matter. The important thing is to maintain the relationship and move forward. Make the client understand that you will work to solve the problem.

Listen, don't interrupt, don't hide or take it personally. Let them vent and let them know that you understand them, and that you will work with them, but don't promise anything that you can't keep.

Of course, all this is also related with active listening, empathy and an attitude of service. You must put yourself in the client's place, with empathy and a real interest in satisfying their needs, with a calm and serene attitude.

Whether they are happy or angry, your clients always expect you to listen to them and to worry about solving their problems.

Many tips can be given to avoid unpleasant situations, but all must start from identifying our own emotions. You must show an attitude of service and a desire to solve obstacles. Analyze what has unleashed the hostility in the client, the real, objective causes, and not persist in opposing positions that only increase the conflict.

In order to avoid the problems that can lead to such a conflict, it is very important to know well how our company works, our product, and understand the real customer experience. Not only thinking that we know all the points and phases of interaction with our company and our product, but the important thing is to know how the client feels in each one of them.

We must not forget that we are people and the sensations and emotions are, rather than logic, which dictate the majority of our decisions. Understanding how it really is, and not how we think that customer experience is, will help us find the points where the client may feel frustrated, lost or deceived. Detecting these defects in the process is a great opportunity to help our client, to serve them better and to avoid any possible argument. There's no need to give reasons for the complaint. In this sense, the best defense is not attack, but to prevent war.

This does not mean that the famous quote "the customer is always right" be a dogma of faith or an undeniable principle. As persons, they may not be right, and nothing happens. There is no need to get into the discussion of who is right. The client may not be right, but he feels that he is, and that is what we should matter to us, and it is our job to find out why this is the case and to do it quickly, because the longer it takes, the greater the distance from the customer and the more difficult it will be to avoid breaking up.

If during the analysis of these causes you discover that it was your mistake, do not try to hide it as if it wasn't. Always apologize to the client, if necessary even compensate them for the error and make sure that with that customer or any other customer, do not repeat the same mistake. Take steps to avoid it and always remember to build and maintain a good future relationship. It's easier and less expensive to keep a customer than to win a new one.

Empathy, active listening, kindness, respect, calmness, control of the situation, cooling of hostilities, knowledge, analysis, quick management, search for solutions, attitude of service and relationship building. But most of all, prevention.

The best discussion is ... the one that never starts.

Tip nº 19. The Non-verbal Communication

"The words are full of falsehood or art; the look is the language of the heart." (William Shakespeare)

We have highlighted the importance of listening, of asking questions and of not arguing with customers, but it is necessary to emphasize that a large part of the communication is also non-verbal, and therefore the salesperson must also incorporate the ability to interpret it as another skill.

Although it is a very extensive topic and there are many books and science on it, so here I just want to talk about its importance, and we invite the curious reader to go deeper into this topic which certainly has much application in the world of sales.

Among other things, it allows us to get to know our clients better, especially in the case of what they do not say, but that they express in one way or another through the body, body language, gestures and tone of voice.

Studies in this regard show that non-verbal language may even be superior to verbal content, having greater weight when emotions and feelings are involved, although the percentage varies widely.

In this sense, the salesperson can apply this knowledge to better negotiate with their clients, discover reactions to the argumentation and proposal, as well as to advance conclusions to react, vary and accommodate the speech and attitude during any meeting.

We all have emotions that when they are intense enough we cannot avoid expressing and that can be deciphered by gestures of the face, lips, eyes, position and body attitudes, etc.

Of course it can also be a great help to understand these emotional signals to get to empathize with our client, understand their deepest motivations and connect better with them.

Body language can tell us a lot about our interlocutor without saying a word. From the way we dress, the distance at which we speak that reveals to us the level of trust, the respect for personal space, body contact, the way we sit and the place where we sit that can indicate a competitive or cooperative attitude, the way we greet each other, the position of our arms and legs as a barrier, the orientation of the body according to our greater or lesser pleasure with the person, the body movement that can be contradictory with the verbal content and show nervousness, restlessness, etc.

The gestures and movements of hands and head when speaking are also often very significant and can show emotional states as well as demonstrate the conviction or not of what the salesperson is exposing.

It is also necessary to point out that there are gestures that mean different things in different countries and that need to be considered, such as the case of moving the head from side to side in India to indicate yes or assent, when in other cultures it is up and down.

Facial expression, gestures and gaze greatly have a great influence on the way we connect with other people and the emotions they arouse in us. With them we also communicate our possible interest, joy, fear, our attention, our displeasure and they serve to reinforce verbal communication and express our emotions.

The frequency with which we look at the other and maintain eye contact can also show interest, liking, superiority, credibility, insecurity, status and many other interpretations depending on the way we look at each other and the length of time that contact is prolonged.

You usually look more when you listen than when you speak, and such eye contact can also direct the flow of dialogue between customer and salesperson and when one or the other has to speak.

The tone, volume and rhythm of the voice can also reveal if we are open to conversation, to interaction, whether we are introverted or extroverted, and they reflect our emotional state, among other things.

Of course we cannot forget the smile that always has a positive effect, relaxes tension, is attractive and ultimately is related with the happiness we have already talked about.

Therefore, it is important that the excellent salesperson goes into these matters in depth, not only to better know his client, but also to better control his movements of arms, hands, gestures, unconscious tics and other messages that do not contribute to his main message and also to be more aware of his own non-verbal signals, which can be counterproductive with our message and our objective of selling.

CHAPTER 4: ON THE COMPETITORS

Tip nº 20. Avoid Competing only for Price

"The supreme art of war is to subdue the enemy without fighting." (Sun Tzu)

In principle, it is essential to know your potential competitors in depth to be able to fight them. Identify if they are really fighting for the same territory, market or clients and investigate who they really are.

Knowing our product well also means knowing the product of the competition well, making comparisons, finding its strengths and weaknesses, knowing what needs they are covering, its basic advantages or benefits for their customers and what strategies they use.

But we do not always need to go to direct war with them, which can lead to an unsuccessful battle for both. You have to find what they do not offer, what market segments they do not cover and exploit their weaknesses.

Especially, we shouldn't compete just for price. It is necessary to add value to our offer to look for advantages that differentiate us, which can only be achieved by knowing the market and the competition in depth. If you're not different or better, you'll have to be cheap....

If what we do is also done by our competitors, it is not differential and it's not going to be a reason to be chosen instead of them, even if we do it well, even if we think our product is of high quality, even if we think we're better. The competition, sooner or later, will make it cheaper. You should not sell or promote the same thing that others sell, that's why you have to constantly watch your competition, not to copy it, but to do it better and to find out how to differentiate yourself.

We have to look for differential values and advantages that the client appreciates. If the client is not willing to pay for it, no matter how different it may be, it is not an added value but quite the opposite. The value of that differential is determined by the customer. It is therefore essential to identify what really concerns them, what they want, to adapt to their requirements and to give it to them in a different way than your competitors do.

Once you have created a link with your clients with a differential product, you can maximize this relationship, sell other products and/or experiment with other niches where there is even more competition, because you will do it from a different position and credibility in that other market. You can also add services to your products, or vice versa, products to your services.

One of the ways to look for differentials is to add ideas to your product, bring intangibles to the table that differentiates it from the rest. Adding new ideas, values and concepts allows selling in new markets, allows differentiation and also to increase the price of the product. It is not always a question of doing better, or cheaper, but of offering different values and advantages than your competition.

One of the current ways to look for those ideas is to add unique experiences to your product or service, experiences both at the point of sale and in the purchasing process or in the way the service is used or consumed. Remember that better than competing on price is competing on service.

One of the current trends is also to use technology and artificial intelligence (AI) to add or develop applications that provide new customer experiences, where there are still a lot of possibilities to explore.

In the following tip we will discuss some ways to differentiate yourself. In this one, the main advice is that you must know your competitors thoroughly to be able to fight against them and avoid competing only for price. It also means getting to know yourself, your product, your company, your philosophy and the unique selling proposition you want to convey.

Tip n° 21. Keys to Differentiate from the Competition

"If you think you're too small to make a difference, try sleeping with a mosquito." (Dalai Lama)

Differentiate! We won't get tired of repeating it. Differentiate yourself and sell competitive advantages. There can be many ways to differentiate, and here we will give you a few hints. The important thing is to understand that competing only for price is suicide and that clients are willing to pay more for differential values that bring them benefits.

This differentiation should not be easily copied by the competition and above all must be profitable, but that is another story that is beyond the scope of this advice.

Likewise, it is essential that this differentiation be communicated correctly and adopted by the client, confirmed as a differential value that the client understands and accepts.

Here are some keys and ways to differentiate yourself from the competition that should be analyzed to adapt them to each particular product or service:

- Different positioning with new advantages and features: it is about adding additional features or advantages to the product that make it unique, benefits that are appreciated by the customer, and focus on that benefit. It is about communicating and highlighting an important feature or advantage that the competition does not have or have not communicated having it. Generally this advantage must be linked to a specific need, motivation, preferences or desire of the client that connects emotionally with them. It may have to do with reliability, durability, safety, technology, material, additives, size, new way of manufacturing that repositions the product, etc.

It can also be related to saving time to the client, removing psychological barriers and minimizing energy and effort for the product purchase and use (see tips 30-33).

This is also closely linked to technological innovation and the launch of new products that seek this differentiation. Being a pioneer with new value-added solutions in business is a differential advantage, creating new markets without having to enter into price war with anyone. There is no need to fight for the same clients and, as we have said, we must look for those market segments not covered by the competition. On the other hand, betting on innovation and creativity is essential today. Those who do not have this business vision will end up dying, as the market is increasingly changing and requires new products and new solutions constantly.

We must also remember that the customer's needs do not change, but rather the ways in which they are met, so that one way to differentiate is to face traditional problems in another way, looking for solutions beyond "the way it has always been done".

Nor should we focus only on making new products, since it is also very important to increase the value of our current services or look for new types of added services as in the next point.

- Level and type of service: A good way to differentiate yourself from your competitors is to offer an excellent level of service. The quality of customer service is one of the values for which customers are willing to pay more. This should include how you make them feel throughout the entire purchase process. I repeat, the whole process. Before, during and after. To follow up post purchase or post service and check if the customer is satisfied is also a point of differentiation that cements the good relationship and helps us to improve, to discover what we are really doing well and what we are not doing and also serving to increase customer loyalty by our interest towards their satisfaction. An excellent service should include the whole process.

Differentiation can also be based on varying the characteristics in which the service is delivered. Warranty can be a form of differentiation. For example, the case of guaranteeing a certain delivery time, a waiting time, product availability, or any other type of service guarantee. Of course, here we must remember that we must not promise what we cannot deliver and that this differential must be demonstrated. The guarantees also have a dark side...

Another way to offer a difference is to provide service through different channels (omnichannel distribution). In this regard, the case of products that have gone from being offered only offline to being offered online is notorious, integrating both possibilities. Innovation in the way the product is distributed can offer many ways to differentiate. If your competition is not present in a place where there are potential customers, it is an opportunity to differentiate yourself with your presence there. Another example is to reduce inconveniences and save time and effort for the customer by bringing the product to their home, their office, or to look for alternative ways of distribution in unusual places.

- Complementary services and products: another way to differentiate from the competition is to create complementary lines of business by offering a global service, increasing the initial base service with complementary services. An example: a hairdresser's where the customer, apart from going to cut or comb their hair, can find an additional service of makeup, aesthetics, facials and body treatments, manicure, pedicure, buy related products, etc. This all-in-one proposal can also be applied to many other markets, products and services.

Another way to increase the service is the type of all-inclusive offers, such as the example of some holiday offers. In the same line, by increasing the number of products instead of services, it is to propose a full range of options greater than what the competition is offering, a larger product range.

- Specialisation: focusing on a specific market niche, less general than that of the competition, is also a way of positioning.

Specializing makes us special and different, less substitutable. Specializing in a market segment, whether in a type of product or service, focusing on a specific group or a geographical area, is for example what offer the luxury cars, cruises for singles, lawyers specialized in divorces, plus-size fashion, services for the elderly, single-country product stores, etc.

This of course requires a deep knowledge and capacity in said market niche that allows this positioning and that transmits the necessary confidence to the client to choose the differentiated option.

Specialisation is also a good strategy for competing in markets dominated by large brands, not by directly confronting them, but by offering a specialised offer, aimed at specific problems with specific solutions that generalist brands do not offer.

Many times, specializing in a certain market niche also allows you to increase your price; there are small segments that are more profitable.

- **Storytelling**: People like to be told stories, stories that connect with the customer and highlight brand values, a message, a lifestyle and experiences that can differentiate us from the competition.

For example, each company may have a unique story about its foundation, evolution, problems, successes, etc., that can be told and on which to base a differential message. Other times storytelling is about positive stories from other satisfied customers or stories around the product that highlight its main and differentiating values. In this sense, don't forget to tell your story!

- **Customer experience**: as mentioned, new experiences make the difference and make the customer purchase memorable. It is not only a question of creating new ways of using or consuming the product or service but also of improving all the points of interaction of the client with the company, increasing their perceived value and their level of loyalty in each and every one of them. For example, you can improve the customer experience by seeking greater convenience in their purchase process, or by increasing the speed of response to any customer inquiry, or by using technological tools to speed up the purchase process. In any case, offering always an experience different from the usual process of the competitors.

Therefore, think about how you can position yourself differently with your product with new advantages and features, think about whether you can differentiate yourself by type and level of service, or by adding complementary products and services, whether you can specialize in a niche market, or add a powerful story to your proposal or whether you can offer a better or different experience to your customer.

Think about it and differentiate yourself. What are you waiting for?

Tip nº 22. Keys to Differentiate from the Competition (II)

"It's not a matter of being better at what you do; it's a matter of being different at what you do." (Michael Porter)

We continue with another series of tips to help you differentiate yourself from your competitors and to help you think which ones are best suited to your particular product or service, apart from those already mentioned above. They are not exclusive and you can also think about mixing several of the aforementioned:

- **Design**: another way to differentiate is to highlight the added value of the design. By varying product design, but maintaining functionality, even small variations that mean something to customers, can lead to competitive differentiation. An example of this is the Apple's commitment to design. The customer is willing to pay more for the same benefits but with a more attractive design. The commitment to design can be transferred to all types of industrial products as well.

It can also be reflected in a different way of packaging the product and new presentations. A new packaging, a different packaging, a different design, even artistic, can be the basis of the differentiation, even if the product is the same as that of the competition. An example of such practices is very common in gift items. Not only is it a matter of emphasizing aesthetics, but the differentiation in the design of the package can be translated into making it more functional, more convenient to use, easy to open, reusable, disposable, etc., or any other aspect that provides differential benefits to the product due to its different design and packaging.

- **Customization**: Another way to differentiate is to customize products with new purchasing processes or offering to customize a product or service in such a way that the result is a unique piece, for which the customer is willing to pay more. An example of this is the customization of clothing, shirts, jackets, etc., with designs chosen by the user. It is also closely linked to the design section we have aforementioned.

- **Exclusivity**: in line with the design and customization ideas, this way of differentiating through exclusive or unique products is another way of specialising in a specific niche, generally with high purchasing power, although it is a concept or purchase motivation that can also be adapted to other customer segments. An example of this is the gourmet and delicatessen products, which transform the level of the product within their market to a more exclusive level, allowing them to differentiate from the competition and raise the price.

- **Quality and Brand**: The brand is a whole that summarizes the value proposition and the expectations of satisfaction, it is our promise to the customer, and differentiates your offer from that of competitors. In the case of similar products, we choose the most recognized brand and/or quality, which give us more security and confidence. In short, in which we perceive more added value. The best differentiation is to connect emotionally at the brand level with customers and at the level of other intangibles such as quality, so that we are in their head as the first choice, or at least within the small list of options that the customer ends up forming in their mind to simplify their decision making. It is about extending the concept of differentiation to the whole company and brand image as a whole.

Investing in brand and quality is another way to differentiate, although not all brands and products get to generate the emotional footprint that is intended to become truly different.

- **Sustainability**: in line with the creation of brand and transmitting brand values, the company's commitment to the environment, to their employees and workers, to their surroundings, to natural manufacturing processes, recycled materials, organic farming, etc., and in general, their philosophy and discourse of being a sustainable business, can also be a differentiating element to achieve customer preference with such a social attitude.

- The salesperson: the good salespersons must know how to differentiate themselves. Businesses are between people, so personal differentiation, generating the client's confidence in your proposal, and the positive perception that you really want to help them can be the decisive and necessary benefit you have to sell, the differential advantage.

You are the salesperson, you are the company, and you are the product. There may be similar products, equals, and companies as well, but like you sure there is no one. The differential advantage can be you, the professional seller, who adds value to the product or service in that market.

In the current panorama where all competing products look almost the same, all perfectly designed to meet the needs of their customers, all with few differences, above and beyond price and brand, it is important to highlight the additional value that can provide the professional salesperson who inspires confidence and security in the customer, becoming the differential value, especially if they are experts in their field. In short, the salesperson is also part of the product and as such can bring additional value with their attitude and skills to differentiate them from the competition.

Betting on differentiation does not always mean having to make radical changes. Sometimes small details are what make the difference, small changes in your offer that are perceived as different. Whichever way you choose, in such a competitive market it is necessary to give the customer purchase reasons that differentiate us from others, giving them new and better options and solutions. The easy thing is to lower the price. The difficult thing is to look for the added values that will allow you to even raise the price.

What are you waiting for? ... Sell your difference.

Tip nº 23. Competitive Benefits and Advantages

"Sustainable competitive advantages no longer exist. All strategies can be imitated". (Michael Porter)

We have talked about differentiating ourselves from the competition as a way of offering and selling an added value that increases the perceived value of our product or service. But we must not forget that we can also sell better benefits and advantages than our competitors. In the first case we avoid frontal combat with the competitor and in the second case we do not. In both cases we try to improve the perception of the quality/price ratio in the client's mind.

As we have mentioned, this means knowing in deep our competitors and ourselves, comparing all those points, characteristics, details, etc., that suppose a benefit perceived by the client and those advantages where we are superior. In fact, all this previous analysis has to be done by the seller and the company before starting to sell, elaborating and working all the comparisons that are necessary and that enrich our sales speech before the normal and expected comparisons of the clients with our competitors. It is necessary to understand their strengths and weaknesses and to confront them with ours.

For the same reason, it is essential to know the market, our segment, sector or niche very well, and to understand its operation, dynamics, main actors, regulations, the previous and current context, what changes they are experiencing and which may come in the future.

In this regard, it is also worth remembering one of the classic tools such as the SWOT analysis (analysis of Strengths, Weaknesses, Opportunities and Threats) to help us choose competitive strategies in relation to those of the competition and the situation of the company in the market. There is a lot of bibliography on the subject that the curious reader can delve into, so we will not insist much here.

It is also important to remember that people buy solutions, not features. To sell is also persuade and the benefits are the ones that persuade customers, emotional and psychological benefits, the ones that provide feelings in the customer beyond the description and the physical characteristics of the product or service. The client does not buy products or services; they buy the tangible, intangible, direct or indirect benefits that our product or service brings them.

The good salesperson always speaks of a characteristic, accompanied by a benefit and an advantage. If only features are shown, the client does not perceive anything. Benefits can close the sale, while just talking about features does not increase the desire to buy.

In short, the client needs to know why he should buy, apart from wanting to know what he is buying.

The key is to find the benefits or advantages that meet the particular needs of the client, and focus on those that really persuade the specific client. All other features, while they may provide desirable advantages to other clients, may not have them for a particular client.

The good salesperson must know very well their product and company, know what benefits, utilities and advantages they can provide compared to the competition, and then find out for each client which can persuade them and which cannot.

Based on this knowledge, the salesperson and the company must define their value proposition and their Unique Selling Proposition (USP), the one that can make you the only option for the client, which makes you unique, the specific benefit that will help you beat the competition by making you preferable. Such a USP must be memorable, to be remembered, appeal to emotions and feelings and help build a long-term relationship with the customer. Customers may not remember how much they paid, or the quality of the product, but they will remember how you made them feel. And this must be included in our USP.

The next step, which is not always done well, is to know how to communicate this USP to customers and make them understand why it is better than that of competitors. Such communication must be done in conjunction with the brand image, so that the USP and the brand define the position and competitive advantage in the market in the mind of the customer.

The USP should not be based just on price, although there can be integrated strategies, combining unique benefits with a price that highlights the differentiation with the competition.

On the other hand, we must think that it is not always the best products that succeed; in fact there are many memorable examples (such as the old case of the VHS tapes versus the higher quality Betamax), so apart from competitive advantages there are other factors that can lean the balance in our favor. One of them is to create habits in our customers, regardless of the quality, advantages and benefits of the product. It is not always the best product that wins, but the one that manages to create the habit of purchase and the repetition of the same in the customer. Being able to create this habit in the customer is one of the best barriers against competition, and can become almost a monopoly of the market. The best example of this we find it in Google and how it maintains its large market share compared to other search engines of the competition.

In this same line, and among many others, we can also mention some other strategies to achieve competitive advantages such as:

- Convince customers to buy more product units and increase the frequency of use of the product.
- Development of new uses for the product.
- Modifications of the current product to conquer new market niches.
- New products that complement the current one or that attack other market segments as well.
- Search for new distribution channels.
- Expansion to other geographical areas: other cities, provinces, regions and also to other countries.
- Acquire (or join) competing companies
- Etc.

Anyway, one of the most important factors to compete today is the ability of the company to adapt over time, so the greatest competitive advantage is the capacity to learn and change quickly to market movements and customer preferences. In short, the new approach to ensuring survival, the best competitive advantage, is to have a vision and perspective of the future that will even lead us to predict it and position ourselves accordingly.

Tip nº 24. Customer Service as a Competitive Advantage

"The excellence of a leader is measured by the ability to turn problems into opportunities." (Peter Drucker)

Although we have already commented that the level and type of service can be a way of differentiation, it is necessary to emphasize that customer service, the superior, is nowadays one of the best competitive advantages as well. In fact, customer service is one of the most influential in the satisfaction and especially in the recommendation to third parties.

It is the best advertising, your customers will recommend you for your good service, for your superior experience compared to the competition and in comparison with their past negative experiences, and therefore, because you exceed their expectations by far, it will be one of the key elements to get their loyalty.

And yet, there are countless companies and vendors that fail at this...

Customer Service, with capital letters, is a key element of the customer experience, and if it's superior to your competition, it's going to be what they remember most, the added value that will make you stand out from the others. The customer will then always compare the service they expects from others with yours, expecting the same from others; you become the reference in their head and that is one of the objectives. Today, customer service is more important than ever among so many undifferentiated offerings.

Reader, ask yourself how others do it, what is the standard type of service, and ask yourself how you can do it better to exceed normal expectations.

The customer service covers not only the support provided after the sale, not only the after-sales service or the attention of claims, but also before that, also in the process of discovering needs and trying to help the client with your experience and advice, answering quickly and efficiently their questions, doubts, concerns and not delaying the developing of your proposal, also consistently directing them throughout the sales process and worrying about solving their problems.

This means that it is likely to rely on several departments, not just the one dedicated to after-sales services, and it means that everyone in the company, from the first to the last, has to be involved in providing excellent customer service. In that sense, more than a service, it has to become a philosophy, in line with the company's culture and commercial policy.

This is also related with what we have already talked about creating more of a long-term relationship with customers than in endeavoring to attract new customers, in achieving a profitable relationship for both parties if we keep them as a loyal customer. We've already said it, but it's good to repeat it: building loyalty with an existing customer is usually more profitable than attracting a new one, and costs on average five times less. In any case, do not neglect either of the two.

It can also be argued that when after-sales service is required, something has gone wrong in the process, in the delivery or installation of the product, or in the use of the service or in the product itself. Of course you have to improve all that so that it does not happen. But experience tells us that sooner or later products fail, break down, a part of the service is not performed as it should be, or the customer needs assistance to get the best performance, best use or any other support required. Of course, the ideal is that everything is perfect, and that nothing breaks the chain of customer loyalty, but when it happens, which will happen (the Murphy's Law, among others...) the best thing is that you are prepared to fix that chain as soon as possible and in the best way, so that this link not only does not break again but becomes the strongest of the whole chain, turning it in a memorable arrangement. It can be an opportunity to surprise the client.

Potential problems with our product or service are sometimes unpredictable. But we can make our response predictable with great customer service, which with the right feedback and analysis of the cases solved will help prevent future incidents and improve both the product and the process.

Many people see customer service as a necessary evil, as an additional cost in the company and even salespeople do not give it the importance it deserves. In their eagerness to sell, they consider that they have already sold and that if something goes wrong, as it also happens to the competition, they do not see it as an opportunity, only as something normal, inherent to the process. But helping and collaborating in providing excellent customer service, before, during and after the sale, is one of the most profitable activities of the company and the seller, it is not an additional cost. It can even help reduce costs if we learn from the experience and data it provides about our mistakes so that we can prevent them in the future.

Many companies even reduce as much as possible their costs and customer service efforts, increasing on the other hand their investment in more sales resources, more salespeople, more products, more marketing, more advertising, etc. Let your competition see it that way...

CHAPTER 5: ON THE PRICE

Tip nº 25. How to Sell More without Lowering the Price

"Every fool confuses value and price." (Antonio Machado)

This tip, in other format and told in a different way, was also part of Smab, but due to its scope and relationship with other tips it is important to adapt it and include it here:

Both companies and sellers should not compete just for price, which is an unproductive battle and we already know how it ends. All companies lose out if they enter the prices war. Price is important in the purchase decision, but it should not be the only purchase reason. The problem is that if we do not have differentiating advantages or if the client perceives similar products or services, he decides only by price. So it is necessary to add new ideas and concepts, to add value to avoid competing only on price. The seller and the company must persuade with a value proposal and add value to their offer, beyond discounts.

Price is just one more variable in the perceived value scales of customers and consumers, and not the only component. The seller must focus on understanding the price beyond its numerical value, and above all understand the true value of the product to customers, the perceived value by the customer.

Perceived value formula: customers always carry out a mental operation to know whether buying is positive for them; to justify the purchase, they make a balance between benefits and sacrifices perceived in the supplier's offer, and the perceived value by the customer is based on the difference between what they receives and what they give:

Perceived Value = (Total benefits + advantages) – (Total costs + prices)

In this formula, the first part is the whole set of economic, functional, abstract, psychological and differential benefits and advantages of the product or service, or added values.

The second term includes all prices and economic costs, and also time, energy/effort and psychological costs (see tips 30-33).

The clients will also make this assessment with your competition:

- If the perceived value of your product is greater than that of the competition, they will be inclined to your offer, and vice versa.
- If the perceived value is negative, the price is the barrier, and generally he will not buy. Or they will say that it is very expensive, they perceives nothing beyond the price
- If the perceived value is very small, the price and the consequent price war may be what decide if they buy from you or from the competition, they will buy the cheaper, or not buy.
- On the other hand, if the perceived value of your product is very high you will sell more.

The value proposal: it is the seller's job to increase this value, making the customer perceives and properly assesses the full set of benefits, including here all the factors and subjective and emotional advantages to counter the price force and rest of negative costs.

In this sense, the price and value of a product are not the same. And so we say that the price is not or should not be the only reason to buy, it is not the only element of the equation, unless we do not make any value proposition.

In short, the value proposition is to explain to your client why they should buy from you and not to your competition

The perceived value is dynamic: the "problem" is that this scale of customer values, this perceived value, is subjective, is abstract and it is a dynamic variable, but not only from yesterday to today, but also from one day to the next. That is, the valuation of the customer is different before the purchase, at the time of purchase, while using the product, and after using the product. There is an initial, middle and final perceived value.

Furthermore, it changes with each client, it is subjective, so for each client or each market segment or niche, you have to make a different value proposal. For the same product, different customer segments perceive different values, and it's something we'll have to play with.

There are also companies that play with the initial and final perceived value, and seek to satisfy their customers by promising them something they can deliver, and then they deliver more than promised or surprise the customer with small details that were not in the initial accepted formula, with values that were not expected. But the opposite is also true, and many promise what they cannot give, disappointing the customer with a final perceived value lower than the initial one, and that is not what we want.

Lowering prices is not the best option: the "easy" part for many companies to comply with this formula is to lower prices, but this does not always mean that demand will increase and also creates another spiral of problems. And it's certainly not the best way to retain customers, who just like come by price, by price will leave. On the other hand, if we want to increase prices it will also be necessary to increase the perceived value of the product in order to raise the price without problems. It is a balance of Price vs. Value. In today's competitive and changing world, the best way is to increase the value of our product and not just reduce prices, if we really want to get to the heart of the customer and get their long-term commitment beyond offers and discounts.

They must buy you because you generate value, not because you are cheaper.

Therefore, companies and salespeople must play with the perceived value of their product in the mind of the customer, which is a continuous work. In addition, customer loyalty, as a result of their degree of satisfaction, will depend on the good or bad management by the seller and the company of this perceived value in relation to the initial expectations. That is, customer satisfaction and loyalty will depend on the difference between the perceived value and their expectations. But that's another story. One that is priceless...

Tip nº 26. The Price Objection

"Man is the measure of all things" (Protagoras)

"It's very expensive", "the price is too high", "it's too expensive", "it's out of my budget", "I can buy it cheaper elsewhere", "if you don't lower the price I do not buy from you"... The price objection is one of the most common and repeated and there is no seller or company that doesn't have to face it. It is the one that arouses the most concern in the seller and overcoming this kind of objections is a daily challenge for sales professionals. It is therefore advisable that we talk and think a little about it.

The matter of price is always important, although more than an objection, it should be recognized as an opportunity to clarify the concerns of the potential client and find out what is really important for them, and why they value the price more than the benefits and advantages that we propose. In fact, it has even been said that the sale begins when the client says "no".

The price objections are often questions from the customer that we must know how to answer, but first we have to find out the question behind it, the origin of the problem. The price objection is usually a smoke curtain from the client to hide their real objection.

On the other hand, discussing the price also means that they are interested in buying (or in paying! ... those who do not plan to pay do not usually discuss it, but that is another story) and should be understood by the seller as such positive signal.

What we should not do when we face a price objection is to lower our offer immediately. The objective is first of all to create value, to increase the perceived value of the product or service. If we lower the price at the beginning, we reduce this value and above all the customer's confidence, who confirms their suspicions that the price might be inflated. Offering a discount or negotiating the price may be acceptable at the appropriate time, but it should not be done in the first place. The first thing to do is always to find the real reason why they are not willing to buy.

Sometimes, price objections are not real, and we must separate those who really have no budget from those who use it as an excuse, not only to lower it but as a way of expressing that they are not entirely convinced.

It may also happen that they do not really appreciate the value of your offer in an appropriate way, they do not understand it, or have the capacity to understand it or we have not transmitted it correctly. In this case it is necessary to show the customer how the product can help them, and how it meets their needs and expectations.

Besides that, you should never take it personally, the price objection is part of the buying process and is a logical reaction in any customer (we do the same thing when buying). It should not be taken as an attack, nor should it be seen as a battle or a haggling. Besides, in such a battle it is not possible to build trust or add value.

Anyway, if you want to sell, if you want to influence someone, tell them the truth. Never lie, especially when it comes to prices.

Although it is not necessary to base the sale on prefabricated answers, it is always good to know some considerations that can help to fight the price objection, and that will be the subject of tips 28 and 29. But first we must remember which is the best strategy, as in the next tip.

Tip n° 27. The Best Strategy to Price Objection

"All our knowledge has its origin in our perceptions".
(Leonardo da Vinci)

The best way to overcome the price objection is ... not to have it. Do not give reasons to do it.

This means being clear that the prospect is qualified to be able to buy, and that we have correctly transmitted the value of our product so that it is higher than the price. Let's talk about these two points below:

- **Prospect qualification**: within the qualification questions (see tip no. 43) the budget must be part of the same in a natural way. It is necessary to clarify at first the price range of our solution (which will generally depend on various options, models, accessories, etc.), or to highlight the most popular option for our customers and confirm whether it fits their budget.

There is no need to initially create a false expectation about the price by indicating a price or price range that is lower than it actually is, regardless of the fact that, once the needs have been exactly determined, the final price or offer be competitive. In any case, remember that if later the prospect does not see the value of your proposal, any price will seem expensive. But it is important to manage the price expectations in advance.

In B2B sales, which are increasingly becoming more long-term, regardless of whether the client seeks the lowest cost, they have to reserve a budget to adjust to, and it is natural that they need to know what we are talking about at the beginning.

In general, the best strategy is to prevent objections from arising, and to do so you need to bring them up during the conversation in a natural and fluid way, being one of the best ways the use of examples from other clients, about their initial concerns about the price and how they finished satisfied.

It is necessary to make a constant prospection that should include those types of customers who do need our product, who will appreciate our advantages, and who will have the capacity and authority to purchase it. Then our job will be to convince and persuade why they should buy from us and not from our competitors, advising as experts in a professional way. In this sense, one of the best defences against price objection is a good prospect qualification. It will also give your sales team more time to focus on those who are most likely to become clients, those who do need what you offer.

Our client will not be the one who looks for other types of benefits and advantages different from what we offer; they will have different expectations and will never be satisfied. If they don't appreciate your benefits, everything will seem expensive to them. Those won't be our client. You have to segment and focus on the right customer. You can't follow and sell to everyone you mistakenly believe can be a customer.

- **Value transmission**: regarding the second point mentioned, the problem is usually that the customer does not see clearly the value of what you sell. If they conclude that the price is too high, they do not feel that the expense is justified.

Possibly the seller:

- Has not previously understood their purchase motivations nor has been able to stimulate them.
- Has not channeled that motivation to convert it into a specific desire of the product.
- Has not increased the perceived value of the product nor has properly managed the expectations.
- Has not transmitted well the values, benefits and cost savings their product or service provides.
- Has talked too much about features that do not provide an inherent value or benefit.
- Has not listened to the client and hasn't asked enough questions to discover their needs.
- Has not accumulated enough value for the customer to make the purchase without price objections.
- Has not generated sufficient confidence in the product, in its quality, or in the seller.
- Has not helped the client.

If this is the case, you have to develop again these additional values, which must be linked to their needs and motivations, and make sure that the client sees, understands and accepts these values. Your product is not valuable in itself, only it is to the extent that the customer perceives it.

Thus, the best way to fight against price objection is to try to prevent it from happening, to qualify correctly and to constantly generate value, so that the client feel that what they receive is more than what they give.

Tip nº 28. Tips and Ideas for Overcoming Price Objections (I)

"Everything complex can be divided into simple parts."
(Descartes)

The following list can give you some ideas on how to resolve price objections with your customers, but always remember that each customer is a world and we have to adapt to each situation, there are no general rules or magic phrases that apply to everything. Common sense must be applied above all. Below, a series of ideas to turn that objection into an additional opportunity:

- **Comparison with the competition**: the customer always compares your value proposal with that of the competition. When a client is asked how they perceive the value of a product, they are actually being asked to compare it to their perception of other existing purchase alternatives. And so a product is not expensive per se, the answer is: "expensive compared to what?" or "too expensive compared to what?" "Expensive" is a relative term. If we find out with what they compare it, we may have arguments to differentiate ourselves and highlight those values that can most counteract this comparison. Value your offer against that of the competition.

Many times it is necessary to make, show, or demonstrate, comparisons that increase the perceived value of our product with respect to that of our competitors. The price of a product is never expensive; if its price is high it is because it is worth it; we should not undervalue the product for it, and we must defend its price with a logical argument of why it is worth more than another of the competition. Knowing your competitors well can avoid hateful comparisons or simply lies based on what the competition offers, strategies that the client can use to lower your price that are not always true, and which defense is based on knowing very well the products and offer of your competitors, prices, economic conditions, advantages, disadvantages, limitations, etc.

If you sell a product which price is higher than the competition's, you need to be very clear about what your differential advantages are and how to defend them, to know in depth the product of the competition and the key and competitive points of your product on which to base your value proposal.

- Why and how much more expensive: a good option is simply to ask why, why is it more expensive? Try to find out how they came to that conclusion, so that they can expose the client's specific concerns, and we can understand their reasoning. This way, by explaining their position, you can make them to reconsider their decision and provide us with data to help them.

In relation to the why, it is good to know how much more expensive it really is for the client, that they really explains the value they have appreciated in our product, the price they considers it is worth and so we can understand their perception and the reason for that perception. Sometimes, knowing "how much expensive" is "very expensive" can help us to effectively overcome the objection. A small additional explanation may be sufficient if it turns out that the price distance is small. In fact, it is often the case that such a distance in price is not so much.

- To agree with the client: it may seem contradictory, but it is a way of supporting that if your product is worth what it is worth, it is because it deserves it, because it is a good product, of quality, and it could not be cheap. It also gives us an additional opportunity to highlight precisely those main points that counteract the force of price. In any case, if your product is more expensive than the competition, and indeed it is, you can do no more than acknowledge it (it would be absurd to discuss it), but from there you have to bring the benefits and advantages that explain the difference.

- Don't answer: silence is sometimes the best answer. There is an old phrase that says that the first one to speak loses, although it is not applicable in all cases, but it is convenient to grant this time of silence so that the clients themselves can express their concerns in a natural way in combination with some of the options mentioned in this advice. Never forget that listening to the customer is the way to discover the real need and work on it.

- Options and alternatives: it is interesting to ask about their other options, mainly not to buy and the negative aspects of not doing so at that time. In this sense, it is advisable to create a sense of urgency, although this should not be a common practice with the same client, since we want to build loyalty in the future and we cannot repeat this type of "pressure" continuously.

Regarding other options, rather than lowering the price, one of them is to offer alternative products, similar products or products that can also satisfy some of the customer's needs that we will have previously detected. In this regard, it is advisable to offer three product options with three different prices, especially if you want them to choose the intermediate option. By having three alternatives (our alternatives, without having to go to look for them to the competition) their price assessment will change as they have several options to choose from. Unconsciously we try to avoid the extremes, neither the most expensive nor the cheapest, so the tendency is to prioritize the intermediate option of the three.

- **Vary the size of the cake**: it is quite typical to negotiate a larger order size if they want to get a better price, increase the size of the cake. For X quantity of product there is a price, which does not change and therefore we defend the price, while for 2X there is another price and it is an alternative to offer. It is not always possible to vary the price by order volume, but it is a possibility to consider as long as it is within reasonable margins for both.

Just as sometimes it is convenient to increase the size of the cake, there are times when it is convenient to reduce it, and if a client does not want to pay the full price or the total value of the product or service, parts of it can be offered at a lower cost, with fewer options included or another product from the catalogue at a lower price. Offer alternatives. Somehow we insist that the price is linked to the set of values and benefits of the product or service and if they want to pay less they have to get less. What do they want to give up? To quality, performance, services, etc., or price?

- **Budget problem**: it is also necessary to find out and ask if it is a budget or payment problem. This is convenient if the customer is asking for a discount, and we need to clarify what is the real objection to be able to negotiate better, as for example the problem may be a temporary cash problem rather than purchase intention.

We always have to thank the customer for their observation of the price, we have already said that it is an opportunity for us to find out more, and one of the things we must find out is what is their budget and ask how much they were thinking to spend. This will give us more clues as to whether the objection is real or not, whether they really have a budget, or whether their decision is stuck with something else.

A radical solution is to ask if the product would solve their problems if it were free. If price is not a problem, it is a way to return to the value, and that the client accepts the possible benefits and advantages. Of course we wouldn't give it away for free, but it's a way to temporarily put aside the problem of price, to later address how to solve the payment method. If there really is no budget, we must try to find alternative solutions to adapt to the one they have. This also means being creative and flexible with our payment methods, to change the client's perspective and fit in with their budget.

- **Trial of the product**: Another way to overcome the price objection when the customer is unsure of the value of your product for them is to allow the trial of said product. This does not apply in all cases and for all types of products, only if the product allows this possibility and if it is confirmed that such practices have a high conversion rate compared to the additional cost it may imply for the company. Therefore, instead of offering a definitive discount, give the client the opportunity to test your product so that they confirm its viability and value for their business or need. Product demonstrations in the B2B market are quite typical (I repeat: if the product allows it) either in visits to the client's installations, at the seller's factory or also at trade shows, presentations and seminars, increasing in this way the client's consideration and perception of the product and clarifying many of their doubts and objections through this trial.

Another way to offer this possibility is through free trial periods, usually short, or by offering some longer periods at a discount, so that after the trial period the product maintains its full price. We thus achieve two things: that the customer validates the usefulness and benefits of our product, recognizing its value at the end of the trial period, and that the customer be happy to have enjoyed that additional extra that he was looking for during that period of time. For example, this practice is typical in digital applications, offering a free trial period of 30 days or similar, which can be extended with another period at a lower cost, to restore the initial price after the trial.

- Compare apples to apples: the potential customer may be comparing with a competitor's product that does not offer the same as ours, one which includes fewer benefits and therefore will always see ours as more expensive.

It is necessary to clarify with what other products they should really compare and change their perception which now can be in line with the real competition. In today's Internet age the clients have the idea that they can buy it cheaper elsewhere, within the reach of a click, but this does not mean that they are buying the same thing. In this scenario it is difficult to compete just for price. It is therefore necessary to look for the values that differentiate us from the competition, to first know what they are really comparing us with, and to highlight our differences and competitive advantages, but this can only be done by comparing products of the same level, quality, services included, etc.

In a creative way, you can also make impossible comparisons of your product with other products that are not related, to make it clear that we need to compare apples with apples, to lead back to the argumentation of values and benefits and to remove the force of the price objection.

- Minimize the price: there is always the option of psychologically minimizing the price, for example not talking about the total, but decomposing it into months or another period of time that decreases the psychological value of the investment. Even at the daily cost, which makes the price much more manageable in the mind of the customer, or for example even in the cost per hour in the case of some industrial products.

The psychological perception of prices is also related with what we have already said about valuing price differently when there are several options on the table. We invite the curious reader to consult the many books and studies on the many possibilities of psychological pricing strategies.

Among all the recommendations I want to highlight one that is less known, applicable to the case of a new product that replaces an older one, and which consists of making the old product more expensive than the new one, thus improving the perceived value of the latest model. Generally the opposite is done, lowering the price of the old model. The concept can also be extrapolated to other situations; it is a question of setting a higher reference price that highlights the value of the one we want to sell, as has been mentioned in the section on presenting options and alternatives. Or on the contrary, you can also offer a lower reference price, but for another product with fewer benefits, as mentioned in the section on the size of the cake.

Likewise, you can reduce the perception of the price of a specific product by packaging it with other products, offering a package of several that masks the price of each one of them.

In this regard, it is also worth noting the lower price perception of some forms of payment where "money is not seen", as is the case of credit cards (or similar payments with mobile phones) or for example the use of casino chips, or at fairs, or the use of gift vouchers and gift cards, etc., which somehow encourage a greater expense by not physically seeing the money.

- **The long term**: you can also make the client think about the long term. It may happen that the client only sees the immediate benefits but not the possible advantages and long-term cost savings of the product or service. In this way, we redirect the price objection to values that the client had not considered. A very extended way is to talk about the possible cost and time savings and headaches in future breakdowns, damage and costs in general to be paid in the future if the product is not of quality and serves to reinforce the value and quality of our product Of course the best thing in these cases is to prove it with figures, with after-sales service statistics, guarantees, etc.

In general, it is a question of bringing the conversation back to the classic difference between price and real cost. The real cost and the price of a product are not the same. The user/customer/consumer will have to incur a series of future costs which may be of various types: repair and maintenance costs, operating/usage costs or operational costs (e.g. energy costs), replacement or durability costs (generally the products do not have an infinite lifetime, and some last longer than others), profitability costs (performance level, real product benefit and proportionality of the investment), product efficiency costs (actual product performance depends on other variables, and cannot always be valued as 100% of its theoretical return), costs of insufficiency (sometimes the product alone does not solve the whole problem and requires other products or additional investment for the client), financial costs (interest on loans for payment, rent, insurance,...), personnel or labor costs associated with the product, etc...

There may be many associated costs, and in each type of product some will be more important than others, this is not intended to be an exhaustive list, it is simply intended to highlight that the customer must be made to think that if they pay or want to pay very little for something, they will eventually discover the reason of such price in the long term when they find other associated costs. This is actually another way to increase the perceived value of the product by explaining or demonstrating how your product can save future costs, in general compared to other alternatives of the competition.

In the same line, it is necessary to ask and know what they expect to get from our particular product or service, which concrete ROI (return on investment) they expect in the long term, to avoid thinking in terms of expensive or cheap and more in terms of benefits and future advantages.

- **The social proof**: another way to overcome the price objection is with examples of references from other clients, who also thought the same thing at first and to show the value that those clients later found, highlighting what they appreciated most, which was certainly not the price itself. The social proof, the testimonies from satisfied clients and referrals are a fundamental tool to reduce the psychological cost that is added to the price and therefore to fight against such objection. Demonstrating results in advance is generally a good way to overcome price objections.

Tip nº 29. Tips and Ideas for Overcoming Price Objections (II)

"In the middle of difficulty lies the opportunity." (Albert Einstein)

We continue with a second series of tips and ideas that may help to resolve price objections, some causes of these objections, as well as some final conclusions:

- **The price objection can be real**: maybe they cannot really pay it. Sometimes, the price objection is real and the potential customer cannot afford your product or service. If this is the case, then it is something to be discovered during the initial qualification and save time for both. That doesn't mean that you don't pay attention to the customer, because they may not have a budget today but they may have it in the future, but it certainly doesn't make sense to try to close a sale today that is not possible to close today. Our goal will change, focusing more on how we can help them today, even if it is not with our product or service, and see how we can educate them in the direction of our solutions. In short, the objective is to build a relationship for the future (see tip no. 39).

- **They are not our customer**: the price objection may be because we are in two very different worlds and they are not our type of customer, but those who will never appreciate the advantages of our product and everything will always seem expensive to them. If our product is not what they really need, it's best to tell them. The client will appreciate the honesty of not wanting to sell them something they don't need, and if they don't become a customer this time, we will have a better chance that they can become a customer in the future when the circumstances change, because we will have earned their trust. We must leave the door open for future opportunities.

- **Decision-making capacity**: it might happen that the price objection is due to the fact that the client is not the one who makes the decisions (it is still an excuse), or that, for example, that prospect is always asked by his superiors to ask for discounts, often without any basis. This is also usual in some purchasing departments, where one of their usual games is to always ask for discounts. They negotiate the price per system and not because they think the product is expensive.

It is always convenient to find out who is the one who really makes the final decision, which is part of the previous qualification phase. This type of price objection can help us to scale up contacts in the organization and clarify which doors we should not forget to touch and understand the real motivations of our interlocutor.

- **It is not the right timing**: a company may have multiple decision makers with different objectives and motivations. In many cases the price objection hides the real objection of delaying the decision until the various departments involved make decisions in one direction or another or until their lines of work coincide in time. In a company there can be many factors that affect such purchasing decisions, such as personnel changes, manufacturing schedules, purchase schedules, new product launches, structural problems, opening new offices or markets, winning contracts and works, etc.

It may not be the right timing to make the decision, since it is linked to other external factors that are yet to come (for example, in personal cases: when I sell the old car, I buy a new one, when the daughter marries next year then I will gift her a trip, if I pass the exam then I reward myself with this,...) so objecting to the price is usually an excuse that masks that inappropriate time, and that they just want to postpone the decision. As we will discuss in the qualification section, it is important to detect when the customer is not yet ready to buy, either because of budget, lack of need or inadequate time.

- Ego, self-esteem and other superior motivations: we must not underestimate the ego of the businessman/woman or anyone, who in order to increase their self-esteem always leads them to discuss the price and somehow "win" the salesperson, whom they see as a rival in their particular battle to buy cheaper than anyone else in the sector.

On the other hand, their experience leads them to believe that the seller's price is always inflated in order to apply later the necessary discount, so they see it essential to discuss the price to obtain the one they believe is fair. It is necessary to overcome this mistrust, this fear of being deceived, and not to present it as a battle, apart from demonstrating and defending what the price of the product really is as a result of the values and benefits, that cost what they cost, and demonstrating that the price is not inflated in advance (here the references of other clients can also help). This does not mean that you cannot have a small offer prepared as a last resort, a detail that can satisfy their ego, always as something symbolic, within our limits, a small price to pay for the establishment of a profitable relationship and not something that reduces the real value of our product.

In the same line of self-esteem, which is a higher need, most people also need to feel that they not only buy cheap things and that they can afford luxuries, whims, or that they can belong to a social class or hierarchy with higher purchase capacity. In short, to make it clear that cheap solutions are not the best and to motivate higher needs that feed the client's ego and self-esteem. You must always show empathy and make it clear that you understand the customer, but at the same time you can ask or find out if they always buy by price. Make it clear that in fact is not always like that, that many of our purchases are not just for price and are related with other motivations.

- **Previous experiences**: It is also important to find out if the customer has previously purchased a similar product or service. It might happen that they really have the wrong idea of what is really worth what we offer. If they do not have previous experience in this regard, it is necessary to put in context and educate the client on what is its real value, which may change the initial perception of the client, who might be classifying the product in a different category.

On the other hand, they may have had negative previous experiences with that product or category of product, a bad memory that results in a lower perceived value in their mind. In that case we will have to find out what happened and understand the cause of the problem in order to be able to argue against that past insecurity and be able to guarantee that it will not happen again this time. In short, find out the real objection behind the excuse of the price. As we have mentioned, customers do not always say the real reasons for not buying, and the easiest way out is to put the price as an excuse, as a defense.

- **The client of your client**: when they are a B2B client, we are always interested in positioning ourselves as a help for the client's business, targeting the client of your client as well, and in that sense it is also interesting to ask them about their products and whether they are the cheapest in their market. We need to redirect the conversation to understanding what values our client needs to sell to their own clients, and what values we should therefore meet or exceed in that goal, thus moving the price issue further away. It is also a matter of turning the idea of a possible expense into an investment for the success of their business, an investment that will help them to sell to their own customers.

- Time to think: if none of the above has worked, sometimes it is convenient to give the client some time to think about it. Give them some time before saying no. Before the client says they have to think about it, we can also suggest it, it will make them feel obliged to reconsider it and reflect for a few days not only in price but on the values and benefits they may lose.

For this, they must be clear and have accepted and recognized these values and benefits as such for themselves. If we have done our job well, applied everything we have said so far, defended our price and our values, if the customer is convinced and persuaded, sometimes it is a matter of waiting for the ripe fruit to fall from the tree. There's a classic saying about it: "you can lead a horse to water, but you can't make it drink."

The next time a client or prospect makes objection to the price, don't get defensive or apply discounts immediately. There is no need to jump directly into a price negotiation process, which anyway creates a precedent for next opportunities and will lead the customer to expect additional discounts in the future. Instead, ask questions, listen, research, redirect the conversation away from the price and focus on how your product or service will benefit the client. You have to ask and find out if the price is the only thing that worries them. As we have commented, there may be other objections that are hidden behind the price objection, and they need to be found out and addressed.

In any case, when dealing with prices, it is always necessary to find out the real needs of the client, to know their real financial situation, to try to sell value rather than price (and demonstrate or justify this value if necessary), to get the necessary confidence of the client towards the seller, find the real causes of the price objection, to provide alternative solutions, always look for the differential elements with respect to the proposal of the competitors, find out who they are comparing us with, and if there is a discount to be made at the end, it should not be free but as a result of a negotiation where both get something, such as increasing the volume of the order, a longer term contract, securing future orders, etc.

In case there is a final discount, it must have a deadline, that generates an urgency to make the deal within reasonable time limits (remember that time kills the offers ... are not eternal)

If there is no agreement, and always thinking about the future, it is also convenient to suggest that this is not the last chance to work together and try to know what other conditions will be necessary in the future to reach an agreement. We suggest that we can adapt the terms but knowing with what conditions.

It is also important to remember that the salesperson must be clear about the company's pricing policy and not hesitate about it. The opposite makes the client feel confident that they are doing the right thing trying to get a better price, and we lose their trust. It is necessary to defend the price and give a good company image, which in turn must also provide a clear pricing policy to the salesperson. Establish in advance which products can never have a discount and which ones can, plan the margins of each product and inform the seller the negotiable limits. The philosophy of the company may also be not to lower prices but instead to offer a gift to certain customers. All this must be planned and scheduled, leaving no room for improvisation so that the seller knows how to handle it in each case.

As a last advice, already mentioned, if they are not your client, your type of client, it is better to let them go, you have to know how to say no and not waste time or effort with those who will not appreciate our product or service in any way or at a lower price. There are problems of the client that we cannot solve. Nor we can sell to everyone. There are also customers who are only interested in buying as cheap as possible, and it is the seller's job to find out if the customer is not willing to pay the fair price of the product.

As we have mentioned, the price objection is not always about price, but often hides something else. It is the seller's job to find out what the real reason is, so that they can deal effectively with the possible solutions.

Tip nº 30. Beyond the Price (I)

"A small leak will sink a great ship." (Benjamin Franklin)

As we have said, it is important to increase the differential values, advantages and benefits to increase the perceived value of the product in the client's mind, but sometimes it is also a matter of reducing costs, and I am not referring to reducing the price of the product itself, nor to minimising the perception of said price by reducing it to smaller periods or quantities or other techniques in this regard, although it is related, especially in the part of the psychological barrier.

We have said that the price and value of a product are not the same. And that is why we say that the price is not or should not be the only reason for purchase; it is not the only element of the equation, unless we do not make any value proposal.

But do not forget that also a part of the costs in the formula is the time used to make a decision or also the time spent in making use of the service, the psychological cost (for example against a certain brand, or stop using the usual product to change to another) and the cost of energy or effort to purchase and enjoy the service. We therefore talk about reducing the second term of the aforementioned equation of perceived value (tip n° 25).

Another discussion is whether the perceived value of an offer can be increased without increasing the cost of production or making major changes in the structure of the companies to carry it out. Sometimes it is not necessary a significant increase in production cost by the producer to reduce these value costs in the mind of the client, and it is only a matter of proposing and seeking solutions that sometimes do not require a great additional effort on our part.

It is not only the monetary cost, and getting the customer to forget the price requires a differential effort in reducing also those associated costs that are not just price in the customer's mind. It is interesting to think about them for a while; we will give some examples in the following tips of this series, although the most productive exercise is to think about your own product or service right now, and try to creatively analyze how to reduce these costs.

Reader, think about reducing or eliminating in your product or service the following negative costs and efforts in the mind of your customer:

- Time costs.
- Psychological costs.
- Effort and energy costs.

Possibly, after that exercise, you can even find a way to raise the price of your product. Definitely, the customer is willing to pay more for a better experience, for a better service, for fewer inconveniences and more security, and for that we must justify and communicate that greater value, which must be really perceived by the customer as such.

Many companies and sellers insist on competing for price, but there will always be another cheaper competitor, so you have to study in depth the needs of your clients and offer other options. It's a matter of rethinking the product and it is worth making that effort to find new solutions, increase the perception of value and that the price goes to the background.

Although you must consider that the client always has the last word and this value proposition must always solve the client's problems, which also change with their situation, their context, their priorities and the type of target client we are addressing.

Tip n° 31. Beyond the Price (II)

"Time is the most valuable thing a man can spend."
(Theophrastus)

> *"It is not that we have a short time to live, but that we waste a lot of it."* (Seneca)

Continuing with this series and going a little deeper into each of the costs suggested in the previous tip, we start with the first one, with the Time Cost:

We can, and should, think of solutions to reduce the time the client spends on their purchase experience, make the product or service more accessible or facilitate the purchase so that it is faster, and therefore favor their purchasing decision. Provide solutions for your clients to buy and decide in less time, make it easy.

For example, this can be translated in providing a quick delivery of the product, or before a promised delivery time, put means so that the client does not queue, does not wait too long, or simply that the customer does not waste time in going to the product, but that it comes to them, eliminating the time of the client's travel. A classic example of this added value is the delivery of food at home, saving time and effort to the client and that today can be found widespread in many other products and services. Today this idea is evolving to such an extent that the trend is to take the entire store to the customer's home, beyond online shopping, using for example the latest virtual reality techniques.

Although we don't have to go to such extremes, and there are many ways to try to reduce the client's time during their purchase process, and make it easier for them, which also has to do with the cost of energy and/or effort that we can and should also reduce.

Sometimes it is as simple as responding quickly to a client's request for quotation. If you take a long time to respond with your proposal, you are wasting your client's time, who will choose the other proposals that came first. The client wants it here and now and they will not wait forever. According to studies in this regard, the first offer a customer receives is also the best valued and the one with the best chance of success.

It is also a matter of analyzing where there is a longer lead time or waiting time for the client in your process and trying to improve it. It can be in the processes of registration of potential clients or contact forms, in the navigation through your website, in the customer service, in the elaboration of the proposal, in the negotiation process, in the administrative process or it can be in the delivery of the product (who has not wasted time waiting for a package?), or it can also be during the use of the product or in its installation. In such use and/or installation we can also think of incorporating elements that reduce this extra time and that may decrease this negative value in the mind of the client.

The use of CRM systems also facilitate the relationship with the client in a quicker way, both pre-sales and post-sales, giving a better and faster customer service, better management of information and customer data in a single place, automating and speeding processes, and can even anticipate the client's needs with better management of similar or periodic orders, etc.

In this regard, another great tool for the salesperson to save time to the client is ... the phone. It sounds unbelievable, but it must be said, because the massive and widespread use of chat applications, computers, technology, multiple round-trip e-mails, etc., make some issues take longer than they should when sometimes they can be solved before with a simple phone call. For better or worse, the phone is still an essential tool for the salesperson and the company.

Looking for ideas to reduce the time cost of client is also about rethinking the location of the product, store or office, and the proximity to the target customer, as well as the accessibility to your product. An example of this is the online bank offers, just a click away, through virtual offices.

It is also related with providing the test or demo of the product in an easy way, which can save the client a lot of decision making time. Many times the client wants to see and touch the product, see how it works, not just see it in the catalog, and it is necessary to put the means to make this possible and not waste time or delay in offering such a demonstration.

Other times, the time saving means directing your client through the steps to follow in your purchase process, have them defined, exposed and planned from the beginning. Don't let the client wait in stages of the process without knowing if it depends on them, if they have to wait for your next communication or if they have to call you. Each previous step should specify what the next step is and how long it takes. For example, if it is required to wait a while for bank approval of an operation or acceptance of a commercial risk to validate a form of payment, you must let the customer know and inform them of this time and process, addressing them to the next step and date, which may be for example the signing of the contract. If the installation of a equipment takes some time, it must be specified, planned in advance with the client and be defined the specific dates. At all times, if we can minimize these waiting times, we will do so, as it is also common for a sale or an operation to be lost due to waiting and execution periods.

There are many examples related with optimizing the time cost of the client, and it would be impossible to mention all of them here.

The important thing is that the readers understand the concept and try to apply it with the necessary creativity to their particular case, to their products or services or to their sales process.

Save time to your client and you'll sell more.

Tip nº 32. Beyond the Price (III)

"Mistrust is the mother of insecurity" (Aristophanes)

We continue this series of associated costs in the client's mind with the important Psychological Cost:

We can call it the negative value of insecurities, because it is much related with trust, sometimes even with guarantees. We are all afraid of being deceived or being scammed. Overcoming this psychological cost can translate for example into guarantees of return and/or substitution (although sometimes the small print of this guarantee and the formalities involved in fulfilling it can be another psychological barrier. We all know of cases where returning a product was a nightmare...), guarantees of repairs, after sales support, finding spare parts, guarantee of delivery time, and in general guarantees that the company or the seller are responsible for any problem.

A classic example of a guarantee that generated the confidence to eliminate this psychological cost to the purchase is the famous slogan: "if you are not satisfied we will refund your money", which has become the motto of many companies, and even in law for online purchases (right of withdrawal when shopping online for a certain period of time). But precisely for this reason, because it has been widely adopted, it is no longer something differential, and it is therefore necessary to look for other differential values with respect to the competition. Although there are products or services and sectors, which are not of a refundable nature initially, where this idea of guarantee could still be applied and it is a matter of thinking about it and deepen into this possibility and conditions to increase the customer's purchasing decision.

Another important psychological cost is that of past negative experiences, which the client does not want to repeat, and that we must find out, understand what problems they had and what problems and fears they want to avoid. It is the salesperson's job to find out about these past experiences, in order to review the offer and combine, in the client's present, their past fears and future expectations with new solutions and values that eliminate this psychological barrier. Just as we have said that we must provide emotional values that persuade the client, positive values, we must also fight against emotional values that dissuade them.

It's all about reducing the fear of making mistakes that we all have as customers. About minimizing the risk.

In this sense, content marketing itself is just other way of overcoming the psychological cost of which we have spoken, by offering content that demonstrates our value, positions us as experts in the sector and increases the knowledge and confidence of the client towards the brand, product or service.

Another example is to provide a proof of authenticity, especially in a world where copies, often fraudulent, are quite common.

It is also very useful to provide the so called social proof, testimonials from satisfied clients and references from experts or customers who have already tried the products and give guarantee and confidence to the distrustful client to overcome the psychological cost to change brand or try a product. Testimonials from happy customers are an essential tool, especially if they are from well-known companies in the sector or from companies similar to those of the potential client, allowing them to see how other companies solved the same problem or even making them see problems that they did not know they had but that this success story helps them to understand.

Ask for testimonials to your satisfied customers and make these references visible, on your website, in your brochures, in your office, etc. Or for example, provide arguments with data and cases that show the advantages and benefits of having two suppliers and not just one, which is a common problem that the seller faces. As we have already mentioned, it is also very important the trust that the seller can generate, as part of the product as well, who must show themselves as expert advisor and clearly show the intention to help the customer, give them security and thus overcome this psychological cost and fear.

In relation to third party proofs to create confidence in the product, we must not forget the typical tests and quality certificates of the various organizations, associations and independent entities, which award their seals of quality and compliance with international standards as differentiating elements, and that provide additional confidence to the product. Examples of this are ISO quality standards, CE marking, protected denominations of origin, etc., or any other type of laboratory tests that may be required of the product.

Minimizing the perception of insecurity is becoming increasingly important, especially now that many relationships are virtual. The client may have insecurity due to many possible causes: in a misinterpretation of the quality or reliability of the product, in the form of payment (e.g. the resistance to paying online, putting our data, bank cards, etc. at risk), in not really having a clear idea of the total cost of the product (e.g.: is transport included in the price?), in thinking that they can find a better price elsewhere, in doubting the real result of the product for their needs, doubts about the brand image in general (we do not trust the unknown brands) and in general in any aspect that involves an additional psychological cost in the mind of the customer, which is added to the monetary price and reduces the perceived value of the product.

It is the task of the seller and the company to investigate these possible causes, find out what psychological costs may exist in each particular case, and once they have been identified, to seek solutions and provide ways to eliminate or minimize these barriers.

Tip nº 33. Beyond the Price (IV)

"The technique is the effort to save effort" (J. Ortega y Gasset)

The last tip in this series is dedicated to the cost of energy and/or effort, which is also closely related to the first mentioned cost, the time cost. There are also many examples in this regard, it is not possible to list them all and for each type of product, market and client there are different solutions and ways to be explored; here we only give some hints so that the concept can be understood and applied accordingly:

The cost of energy and effort of the client can be called the cost of discomforts. Inconveniences and disadvantages that can suppose more to the client than the price of the product itself. In fact, there are many customers who would be willing to pay more if such inconveniences were eliminated. A good customer experience also depends on offering experiences without effort, without barriers. Trying to reduce the cost of energy or effort to the client can be translated into improving the ease and accessibility to obtain the product or service.

Some examples are: a wide opening hours, a secure parking space, access to online purchase or online operations, easy access to your product from the mobile phone (many online stores are not yet adapted to mobile devices), or a good distribution of points of sale and proximity to the customer in general that avoids the customer having to travel excessively wasting energy, effort and time. It is also about simplifying purchase processes, which do not require multiple steps, but the minimum possible, avoiding bureaucracy, paperwork and unnecessary travel to the client, etc.

Going deeper into this area can also lead us to offer additional services that have an impact on reducing the customer's efforts, such as a product installation service, or reducing the training required for its use with training videos on the subject, a course, clear and simple user or installation manuals, problem reports and solutions to get the most out of the product, etc.

It is important to look for the questions that customers ask during their shopping experience and try to answer them in advance by offering information in different formats, such as videos, technical notes, articles, instructions for use, guided purchase, etc., that will help them to overcome this additional effort and clarify their doubts as soon as possible.

Sometimes reducing the effort is as simple as speaking the client's own language. Not only do I mean that your product must have the information in the language of the country where you want to sell it (it is usual to find information and user manuals in other languages except yours). I also mean that your message must be easy to understand, in the way the client speaks (for example, sometimes it can be too technical) or to say it in different ways, to provide a clear message that does not lead to mistakes. The misinterpretations by the client are translated into wrong value perceptions simply because the message requires additional effort by the client to understand it, especially if the message is very long and unclear.

As in the psychological cost, the professional salesperson must also be another element that saves energy and effort to the client, advising them on the best solution and not wasting time. If we can't help you with our product, the good salesperson will tell it to them and will try to bring some kind of additional value to help them solve their problem or need, helping them in their search and building a relationship of trust that will be worth when they do need our solution.

It is also advisable to reduce the effort of the customer in their search for information by providing answers to their frequently asked questions and doubts, which may include not only the availability of the typical FAQ list but also that all information required by the customer about your product or service be available and easily accessible in a documentation center that allows the search for information quickly and efficiently, and if possible, with personalized attention. In this regards, chat type applications have become quite widespread where even instead of an agent, chatbots are being used; but we must never forget the human element that the customers require, who must always have this option available.

In short, and finishing the comments of this series of tips, it is a matter of thinking about everything that can reduce the effort of the client to make the purchase decision and for the use and enjoyment of the product. To eliminate barriers that, as we have said, are usually of time, psychological and of effort or energy. In this process we can convert values that were initially negative into positive values that add up in the initial and final perception of our offer.

In any case, all these values are worthless if we do not communicate them. Many times we simply have added values, competitive values, but we do not realize it and we do not share these values with the client. The problem sometimes lies in knowing how to transmit it or finding the right means to do so. You cannot perceive value if you do not know it. If you have a special way of doing things, you should let your customers know. Make tutorials, articles, webinars, interview your satisfied customers, suppliers, show your company inside, etc.

By last: always keep your promises! The problems come when we do not fulfill the promise, when there is an imbalance between the initial perceived value and the final perceived value, since we must not forget that they can be different. On the contrary, if we give more than we promised, then you will not only have satisfied customers, but it will also be a factor to increase their possible loyalty.

CHAPTER 6: ABOUT THE CUSTOMER EXPERIENCE

Tip n° 34. About the Customer Experience

"We see our customers as invited guests to a party, and we are the hosts. It's our job every day to make every important aspect of the customer experience a little bit better". (Jeff Bezos)

There is much talk about the customer experience. All companies and brands talk and boast of providing a great customer experience. In fact, it is one of the most frequently mentioned terms in the current digital transformation of business. But what is the customer experience?

There are many definitions, but among many others I like this one (from the Spanish version of Wikipedia): "customer experience is the product of a customer's perceptions after interacting rationally, physically, emotionally and/or psychologically with any part of a company. This perception affects customer behavior and generates memories that drive loyalty and affect the economic value an organization generates."

The key words here are "perceptions", "memories" and "loyalty". We will insist on them throughout the following paragraphs and tips.

We have said that customers buy for emotions that they justify with logical arguments, so one way to influence their decision is to provide the experience that generates the desired emotion towards our product, and this is also part of the overall experience of the customer, user or consumer with our company.

Managing the customer experience means increasing the customer's perceptions of value, optimizing customer's satisfaction, meeting their expectations and exceeding them if possible to gain their loyalty. It is about optimizing the different processes, the different touchpoints or customer interactions with the company.

It is important to highlight that it is about all interactions, and therefore it is broader than just the user's experience with a product. Nor is it limited to customer service, which is included in the experience if the customer makes use of it. Commercial and marketing actions are also part of this experience, but it is still broader, even when the customer, for whatever reason, stops using your product or service. It includes from the first contact with the company to the last one, valuing the perception of the client, their subjective vision, in each and every one of them.

As mentioned, there is much talk lately about the customer experience and how to optimize it. Casually, or causally, many of the keys mentioned in Smab, and extended here, are also the same to improve that customer experience:

- **The emotional factor**: emotions sell and therefore also impact the customer experience. We remember the experience mainly by our emotions about it, emotions that connect with your brand, product or service.

- **Differentiation**: it is necessary to differentiate yourself from the competition in order to sell, and so it must be the differential competitive advantages that produce the customer experience, not the common advantages, we must not insist on offering more of the same. The customer experience must be different than that of your competition. On the other hand, this differentiation is not only achieved with discounts or offers.

- **Reduce non-monetary costs**: the time, effort and psychological costs are added to the price and reduce the perceived value of our product and consequently the customer experience. Make it simple. The way for the customer to enjoy your product or service should not be complicated. You may have a great differentiation and be able to excite emotions but you will not reach the client if they have to put a lot of effort into it to appreciate your customer experience.

- **The empathy factor**: look at the experience from the client's point of view, or rather experience it for yourself, you may be surprised that theory and reality can be very different...

- **Listen to the client**: ask them about their experience and how to improve it. It is also necessary to make it easy for the client to give their opinion about their experience, to have a place where their voice is heard. Value their opinion, and even reward them for giving it.

- **Respect the customer**: in general, with all that this means, value their point of view, their experience, their perception, look through their eyes, recognize your mistakes and solve the possible problems. Nothing more, and nothing less.

The customer experience is here to stay. Nowadays it is essential to study, analyze and optimize the customer experience with your company. Specific positions have even been created in many companies, with professionals specialized in customer experience. And you ... are you taking into account the customer experience in your business?

Tip n° 35. The Customer Experience (II) - the Perceived Value

"Don't judge a man until you have walked two moons in his moccasins (Sioux proverb)

We said that the perceived value of a product by the customer is subjective, abstract and is a dynamic variable. The customer's valuation is different before the purchase, at the time of purchase, at the time of its use, and after its use.

There is an initial, middle and final perceived value of the product. It also changes with each customer, market or niche. For the same product, different customer segments perceive different values.

Similarly, the customer experience includes all the different perceptions of the client regarding the company and/or brand in their interactions with it (and this includes not only the salesperson, but also any other employee of the company). The customer experience goes beyond the perceived value of the product and beyond the client/salesperson relationship, but of course it also includes both.

We could say that the customer experience is a sum of all the different individual perceptions or perceived values by the customer in each stage, on each occasion of contact with the company, on each occasion of contact with the product, with the brand, with its associated staff, with its sales staff, with its sales processes, marketing, social actions, advertising, service, etc.. The set of all these unitary perceived values, extrapolated to the whole company or brand.

Like the perceived value of the product, this vital experience of the client as the sum of their perceptions is also subjective, abstract and a dynamic variable.

It is subjective because each customer has a different image of what their ideal customer experience would be. Your company may think that its products are of high quality and that they offer a good experience to the customer, but if for example a customer complains about a product, receives bad attention, or both, their perception is that neither the company nor the product has such quality, and that perception is the reality that matters to us, the only reality, not the one the company think it is.

It is abstract because it is based on memories, emotions and psychological aspects apart from physical and rational interaction. That does not mean that there is no possibility to measure and control it. In tip no. 38 we will talk about some of the tools that exist in this regard.

Likewise, the customer experience is dynamic because such perceptions, memories and loyalty to the brand vary throughout the customer's journey, along the life cycle of the client. A client may have a bad initial experience with some company, but if later that company has managed to solve the problem successfully, with excellent service or other details that leave them with a good memory and taste, the customer may end up concluding that they would repeat the experience and even that they would recommend it to others, they may end with a good customer experience.

It is therefore important to value this customer experience in each and every one of the interactions along the famous sales funnel. We are obliged to improve it and thus achieve a general increase in the values and perceptions of the customer towards our company, which will result in a long and fruitful relationship that will lead to the loyalty of our customers, in the same way as it resulted when increasing the perceived value of the product.

Take the time to make sure that every step of the client's journey is solid, that it will create good perceptions and increase the probability that customers will come back and tell their friends about your business. But you have to be careful, the perception of the client is fragile and can change with each interaction, so you have to try to maintain a good customer experience without ups and downs, it is a constant job.

Tip nº 36. The Customer Experience (III) - the Influence on the Brand

"Only the one who loves your soul loves you" (Plato)

As we have said, the customer experience is based on perceptions, memories, values and loyalty. This customer experience is sublimated in the final perception that the client has of your brand. In that sense I think it is interesting to talk a bit about the customer experience and the brand.

The brand is a whole that summarizes the value proposal and the expectations of satisfaction. In today's competitive world we have gone from selling products to selling sensations, solutions and ideas beyond the characteristics of the product, we sell experiences.

The products are increasingly similar, they are all similar in quality, and it is difficult for customers to distinguish them by their attributes, so it is necessary to associate them with an experience, an emotional image, a maximum value that satisfies their needs, an idea, a philosophy, and often a positive story. Perceptions, memories and loyalty.

Optimizing the customer experience also serves to build brand image, helping to create the emotional footprint necessary for that brand to be maintained over time, so that the experience is evoked by the clients in their memories, emotions, perceptions and image of said brand.

The company creates a customer experience which is consistent with the emotions and memories they want to set and fix in the customer and consumer, and then these emotional triggers end up becoming unconscious signals, which become part of the brand.

The brand itself ends up evoking these experiences. The customer experience ends up becoming a brand experience. One leads to the other, and finally the other way around.

Today, building a brand is no longer an option, it is a necessary condition to attract, connect and excite the consumer. Similarly, offering successful customer experiences today is also not an option but a need, being essential to differentiate yourself from the competition. The client are increasingly globalized, have got a lot of information, requires some identification with said maximum values and wants also to find some differentiation among all the noise with good experiences.

Definitely, offer satisfying, memorable, unforgettable customer experiences, and you will build your brand.

Tip nº 37. The Customer Experience (IV) - The Loyalty

"Do what you do so well that they will want to see it again and bring their friends." (Walt Disney)

Coming back to one of the initial keywords, loyalty, the point and target is to optimize that loyalty by improving the customer experience.

Loyalty is a matter of emotions, and that must be the added value of the formula in our favour. Therefore, improving the customer experience also means creating this attitude and psychological connection along with the sufficient motivation to produce the repetition of the purchase.

The fact is that the customer satisfaction is not enough. All brands can have satisfied customers. At the other hand, today almost all the products end up being similar and all the brands look the same to us; the competition is extreme, they copy each other, and it is difficult to find differential characteristics and advantages; we already know that when the customer perceives similar goods or services, they compete only for price.

In this situation it is necessary to go further, and to offer new perceptions of value, new experiences. The customer experience has to do with emotions, as we have said, and are these emotions and these new experiences that are developed to offer the customer that differentiation that lead them to increase their satisfaction and ultimately to achieve their commitment, their loyalty. The new target and ultimate goal is to turn customers into fans through memorable experiences. From "consumer" to "fansumer".

Programming a good customer experience should also start with a proper understanding of the changing clients's expectations. This also requires to keep a constant communication with them in order to know what these expectations are at all time; then, those expectations must be reflected at each and every one of the touchpoints with the customer; but above all, it is essential to eliminate or change those events that do not meet those expectations, not only below but also above.

A big mistake is to promise more than you can deliver, and to generate exaggerated expectations in your efforts to sell more. If there has not been an increase in the value of the product, the result is customer dissatisfaction, so that a correct level of expectations must be established from the company and the seller.

So, to increase customer loyalty you have to add benefits and added value throughout your experience, differential advantages, if possible emotional ones, reduce costs and barriers that decrease the perceived value of that experience, and make sure that the experience is greater than the expectations created, which have to be consistent with what we can offer.

Tip nº 38. Customer Experience Tools

"He who knows all the answers has not been asked all the questions." (Confucius)

Based on the above, multiple tools and methods are developed to analyze and understand the customer experience, design and improve it in all the processes involved and integrate it with the business model to offer the customer the maximum value with a good experience. It is necessary to know which points of interaction and which phases of the relationship with the client should be improved so that clients have better experiences that lead to loyalty. The stages to improve can include anyone of the whole sales process.

The problem is that any point of contact matters and it is difficult for the company to maintain consistency across all these points of contact. The chain of loyalty has many links and can be broken by any of them. It is necessary to use different tools as we have said to analyze, coordinate and optimize the weakest links, the most relevant points of contact and those that can produce a bad customer experience.

Examples of such tools are:

- Customer Journey Mapping (CJM).
- Customer lifetime value.
- The Sales Funnels.
- Analysis of customer behavior and metrics.
- Developing and representation of ideal clients (Buyer Persona).
- Customer satisfaction surveys and analysis.

- Measurement of customer loyalty to a brand according to its probability of recommendation (Net Promoter Score).
- Customer Effort Score (CES)
- Customer empathy maps.
- The Blueprint for service design.
- Social Listening and analysis of engagement metrics.
- Optimization of navigation and accessibility to information (both on the web and from mobile phones).
- Online chats to help and guide the purchase.
- Management of the knowledge of the company.
- Analysis of speed, quality of service, complaints, etc.
- Analysis of the happiness of your sales and customer service team.
- Automatic order tracking.
- Customer service platforms in social networks.
- Multi-channel communications with customers.
- Predictive Technology or intelligence of trends and suggestions to the customer (and other multiple tools for analysis of Big Data and Small Data to know the customer in a comprehensive way).
- Business tools for innovation from the design and remodelling of the product that provide solutions to the needs of users (Design Thinking)
- CRM itself, whose many advantages help us to improve the customer experience and our relationship with the customer.
- Etc.

It's also interesting to highlight the increasing integration of artificial intelligence in each and every one of the processes and interactions with the customer. One example is the use of chatbots as an automated customer assistant. But we must never forget the danger of dehumanizing the sale. The customer ultimately requires human contact, and the whole process cannot be left exclusively in the hands of robots, there must be a balance of both.

The curious reader can deepen into all these tools, the scope of which is beyond the target and extension of these tips, as there is a lot of information and books about it.

The important thing is to understand and assimilate that we necessarily have to invest in some of the aforementioned tools to improve the customer experience and thus gain their loyalty, get they repeat purchase and that they recommend us.

Tip nº 39. The Prospect Experience

"Be kind, for everyone you meet is fighting a harder battle."
(Plato)

We've talked about improving the customer experience, but that experience starts from the first contact with the company or salesperson, from the time they are a prospect, not just when they become a customer. It doesn't start when they sign the contract, but from the first time you contact them. In that sense, the experience of the prospect is not usually very good. Nobody talks about the prospect experience, and it is necessary to vindicate it and make the whole sales process more friendly with them.

Let's take a well-known example: who has not seen the film "Pretty Woman"? I'm sure we all remember it, and we may have seen it more than once. Surely the reader will remember that scene in which Julia Roberts goes to a fashion boutique, dressed in her own way, and with the need to buy a dress for her date with Richard Gere that night.

In this scene, the store clerks arrogantly classify and qualify her for her appearance and practically kick her out of the store. They qualified her as someone who's not going to buy from the store, who's not going to be their customer. She returns distressed to the hotel, not only because she could not buy despite having money, but because they had not treated her as a person. She had been declassified as a potential client at the store.

We also remember the scene that happens later on where she returns to the same shop, well dressed and with many shopping bags in her hand. She bought at another store, another one where she was treated better. Challenging, she rebuked the saleswomen who didn't help her, showing them her big purchase and showing them the commission they had missed ... But in reality that usually doesn't happen, the customer doesn't come back to tell us that he or she has bought elsewhere. We just don't know about it.

That is the experience of the prospect on many occasions. The marketing and sales process qualifies the prospects and when they are not going to be an immediate customer they are sent to the CRM background in the best of cases as another cold lead, and in the worst they are never contacted again by the seller.

On the one hand, we want the seller to be a trusted advisor, but on the other hand, if the prospect is not ready to buy, for any of the reasons we will discuss in the BANT method for qualifying opportunities (tip nº 43), or for any other, if it is not time for them to enter our sales funnel, the prospect is simply ignored, the seller does not advise or listen to them, or give them any value.

The prospect looks for trust, wants to buy from someone they can trust. They expect that every time they contact a supplier they will offer value to them, understand their problems, and they do not want to be qualified or sold (remember that "people love to buy, but hate to be sold to", and therefore, similarly, we don't like to be qualified either) but we only give them value, confidence or we are interested in talking to them if they have money to spend today. They cannot trust us when we have decided that the potential customer is not ready to buy and we lose interest in them. The day they're ready to buy, they won't call you, they'll buy someone else.

In this sense, it is necessary to have a balance in our dealings with the prospect, to offer something of value to them in each interaction with the potential client, something that, although not immediately translated into an order for the seller, build a bond of trust, so that the seller and the company are established in the mind of that prospect. In such a way that, in the case of one, or two or several months, or a year, or whenever the prospect is ready to buy or plans to buy, when the opportunity is combined with the need and the means, then the name of that seller or company is the first in their head.

Giving value to the client starts by listening to the prospect from the very beginning of their experience. And trying to help them, even if it's not with your product that day. Maybe it is by introducing them to someone in the sector, to another customer, or with technical information that may be useful for their business, or by advising them on their options, answering their questions, even discouraging them from buying our product because at that time it is not for them, or simply by showing our interest in their problems and our desire to help. In the future it will also be convenient to share special content with the prospect, which can be customized or adapted to the specific situation of the potential client, anything that speaks directly to the client's motivations and interests, making them feel that what we provide is worthwhile.

On the other hand, we must never forget that this prospect, as with a customer who has already bought, can refer and recommend us to another potential customer, and can speak well of us, even if they have not yet bought and do not know how it is the experience with our product and company. But they will have felt their good experience as a prospect, because we will have listened to them and treated them as a person, and they will remember that.

In short, it's about treating your potential customer or prospect with respect, or in other words, the way you would like to be treated.

Today's B2B sales are becoming increasingly complex and longer. This makes even more necessary to focus on creating long-term value relationships that will eventually turn these prospects into customers.

According to the latest statistics, only 3% to 6% of prospects are ready to buy at the first contact with the supplier. Today this prospect may not have a budget, a need, or that is not the right time, but maybe they will have some of these elements in two months or six, so that what is important to us is not to forget to that vast majority (more than 94%!) of potential buyers.

We must educate these prospects, these potential customers throughout the whole process, starting from our first contact with them, maintaining regular contact that today can even be done in an automated way, through various social networks (Linkedin, Twitter, etc), company blogs, newsletters, email campaigns, user forums, etc.

The goal is to make our product or service more compelling to a potential customer by demonstrating our value proposition in a transparent way and generating the confidence that we really understand their problems and share their objectives. We have to show ourselves interested in the success of our clients and cultivate a mindset of being a partner, rather than just a supplier or vendor.

Thinking again about the aforementioned statistics, today it is more necessary than ever to establish means to stay in the customer's mind as a potential supplier and we cannot do that if we dehumanize the sale and treat them as in the example of the film. Today, the prospect experience is just as important as the customer experience.

The success in education of the prospect will come with the constant effort. A buyer may not be ready to decide when you contact them for the first time, but through sustained contact you can cultivate their interest and develop your credibility as a seller.

Prospects want to talk to real human beings before they are ready to buy, and to deal with experts who add value beyond their products. This can only be done by educating these prospects in our solutions, providing value in each interaction with them and building a relationship of confidence that positions us as a reference for when they can buy, when they have a need or when they can no longer delay in solving what we can solve.

Precisely, this is one of the objectives of the growing Inbound Marketing, which focuses on educating potential customers through useful and quality content through articles, webinars, reports, blogs, social media actions, personalized content marketing, etc., to generate interest from the potential customer to the company and products, less aggressively than with direct marketing, and trying to make the prospects advance faster through the sales funnel.

The salesperson in this sense must contribute his knowledge as an expert to lead the customers and prospects to their solutions throughout the whole process, providing a more efficient buying experience and providing the guided and consultative sales part necessary to facilitate this experience (tip no. 4).

Build a good prospect experience and don't just focus on the customer experience. Build a bond of trust from the beginning, cultivate it constantly and the sale will just come.

Think what would have happened if Julia Roberts had been treated in a different way in that first store.... Even if she hadn't bought that day, she would have eventually returned to that store. But she didn't shop there again, she chose another store, and that's what happens many times in reality, and not just in the movies...

Final note: the same applies to failed sales and lost opportunities. Don't burn the bridges with the customers you didn't get to close. Keep them close and you'll learn why they didn't buy from you, they will help you to improve and possibly they will buy you in the future if you build a quality relationship. Even if they don't buy you today.

CHAPTER 7: ON PROSPECTING

Tip nº 40. Generating New Opportunities - Prospecting

"If one does not know to which port one is sailing, no wind is favorable." (Seneca)

Prospecting is the first part of the sales process. In general, prospecting involves a search (supposed to be organized, another thing is that many companies do it in a disorganized way) to identify and reach potential customers or prospects. The salesperson must always dedicate a significant portion of their time to this task, because they can't just stop in selling only to current customers.

There are many books, blogs, courses, seminars, etc. on the subject and we will leave the curious reader to investigate deeper into what can be more interesting for their particular business or product, so here we will only give a few hints on the subject. Thus, broadly speaking, we can define three stages in the prospecting process:

- **Definition of potential/ideal clients (tip no. 40)**
- **Searching for potential clients (tip no. 41)**
- **Qualification of prospects (tips no. 42 to 44)**

Let's start with the first one, and also by clarifying the concepts of prospects and leads, which we find in a generalized way and it is convenient to review them to better focus our process.

- **Definition of potential customers:** it is essential to define and identify our ideal client first. For this it is also important to know our product in depth, as it will be the advantages and benefits of said product or service that define that ideal client. If we know our product well we will know our ideal client and vice versa.

It is just as important to analyze the competition. If we study the competition we are also analyzing our potential market, market segments that need our product or service, and identifying market niches that we can attack, either directly or indirectly, covering needs that are not covered by the competition.

It is also essential to know the needs that we seek to satisfy and the purchase motivations that we can stimulate to know better the potential customers of our product and to segment in an adequate and effective way to reach our ideal customers. Divide and conquer, as the Romans said.

In short, we must analyze who really needs what we offer to be potential customers. Or we may be pointing in the wrong direction, and trying to attract customers who are not the ones we are really interested in, a waste of time, effort and money.

You can't chase and sell to everyone you believe can be a customer. That's why you have to segment and focus on the right client. And if they are not our kind of client, let them go.

One of the mistakes that sellers and companies make is not correctly identifying some or all of the characteristics of their ideal client, so this stage is particularly important and will have very serious consequences later if it is not done or not done properly.

- **Prospects and Leads**: we can then understand the prospect as a potential client who belongs or should belong to our ideal client segmentation, who may become a customer, user or consumer, and who may initially be interested in our product, even if he or she has not yet expressed it. We consider prospects those companies or potential clients that are simply part of our target market, our "buyer persona" (archetype of the ideal customer of a product or service). A prospect can be converted into a sales opportunity.

The prospect is also understood in some industries and contexts such as the one that has already had a contact or conversation with the salesperson and is at a more advanced point in the sales funnel. In both cases a prospect is a "suspect" to become a client, a potential client. It is the seller's job to confirm that suspicion throughout the process by searching, identifying and then contacting and qualifying that prospect in order to generate opportunities.

On the other hand, there are also the leads, those who have shown or expressed an interest in us, either by filling a web form to receive more information, or contacting us by other means and we have confirmed an interest in our company or product. In short, a lead is a person who has identified and shown interest in your product or service in some way.

Both are potential customers, both prospects and leads. Broadly speaking, we can understand leads as potential customers who contact the company (whether through calls, forms, marketing campaigns, etc.) and have already expressed some interest, although they still have an indefinite sale potential. Depending on the context and the industry, many consider the prospect as a step above the lead, so that the lead when it is qualified becomes a prospect, and they call it "Sales Ready Leads", so that a prospect would also be a lead prepared for sales, apart from being also those potential customers who have not yet shown interest and that our sales team contacts proactively.

There is a lot of discussion about what is considered a lead and a prospect. But we are not going to get into this debate, nor get lost in semantics, the important thing is that the curious reader simplifies mentally and is left with the idea of a potential client which is what interests the salesperson.

Thus, from the salesperson's point of view, they can handle two types of prospects with the target of turning them into opportunities:

- **Prospects generated from leads**: it can happen that this lead, without nurturing, passes directly to the salesperson, which is common in many small and medium companies where there is not a differentiated marketing department, or even having it, that a percentage of these leads go directly to sales (as may be the case with direct requests for quotations or RFQs). Or they can be leads that have "matured" enough to be processed by the salesperson, and have gone through several lead qualification phases from the marketing department (sales ready leads), but still have to go through the phase of prospect qualification by the salesperson's action.

- **Prospects generated by the salesperson**: they can come from cold calls or emails, from prospecting visits, from contacts at trade shows, congresses, seminars, networking or social networks of the salesperson, proactive actions of the salesperson, etc. These are prospects who must also go through the salesperson's qualification phase.

There must be a consensus between marketing and sales on what they both consider a lead or a prospect, a common idea of how both should treat it and when it is the responsibility of one or the other department. But this depends a lot on the type of industry, market and type of product or service, and even varies according to the concept applied by each CRM, so we will leave it to the curious reader to further investigate in that aspect if interested.

On the other hand, it is also important to consider that in B2B what can start with a single-person lead is often turned into a multi-prospect opportunity, or even into several opportunities with different responsible prospects, since there are usually many people involved in decision making, several contacts in a department, different departments, different delegations, different purchase projects for different products, etc.

Having said that, the next step is to qualify those potential clients or prospects. Depending on that qualification (if they meet several criteria such as those of tip n° 43), in many CRM systems they would be assigned as a new opportunity contact. Or not, they can stay in simple prospects and not move or become opportunities. They may not even consider your proposal, even if they have a need, budget and other criteria, or they may only be gathering information without the other criteria being defined. Other external problems are also frequent, such as staff changes, project changes, etc. that sometimes cause a prospect to not become an opportunity. If that opportunity ends in a purchase, in closing a sale, it would be a conversion. The conversion rate, or proportion of leads and leads that are converted into sales, is one way to measure the effectiveness of the sales process, sales team or salesperson.

The main advice for the curious reader is to be clear about the great importance of prospecting throughout the sales process, and to analyze each and every one of the phases of prospecting that we have indicated.

It is therefore necessary to qualify potential clients, whether they are leads or prospects, on the basis of certain criteria. But first we will talk about the search for potential clients, which is the step prior to the qualification.

Tip nº 41. Searching for Potential Clients

"If you look hard, you will find." (Plato)

Based on the above, we can consider two main groups and activities of search and generation of potential clients:

- **Leads generation:** mainly through Inbound Marketing (which will later become prospects)
- **Prospects generation:** mainly through Outbound actions of the sales team.

In this regard, there is a lot of discussion about whether the Inbound actions should be greater than those of Outbound or vice versa or how they should be combined. It even goes so far as to say that you should only have to attract potential customers, not go and look for them, but this will depend a lot on the industry and the product. The normal thing is to combine and integrate both solutions, trying to improve the filtering and processing of inbound requests together with a better approach of proactive activities towards potential clients that coincide with our ideal client. Not everything has to be just attraction marketing and the need to actively prospect remains fundamental.

Anyway, in today's increasingly complex and varied B2B sales environment, there is no one perfect or universal way to manage every single sales opportunity or a solution that fits every case and every context.

Within that search for potential customers there may be more sub-phases, such as:

- Identify the company.
- Identify the valid contact(s) in that company, positions in that company, responsibilities, etc.
- Identify telephone, email, address, etc. of those contacts.
- Evaluate their potential as a client.
- Bidirectional communication that goes deeper into the previous aspects. Pre-qualification questions such as: Is it the right company? Is the contact the right one? Has any need been identified that we can address?

The above is valid for both leads and prospects. In the case of the initial lead generated by marketing, for example through a form, we can have minimum data, but if we manage to advance in these sub-phases we can have a qualified lead for sales or prospect (if and only if marketing and sales agree on what level or phase that lead can be considered as ready for sales). The stage at which a lead will be considered ready for sales will vary from one industry to another, so it is the task of each company to adapt it to their convenience and resources.

Even if the prospect has been generated by the salespeople, the above details must also be identified and all the necessary information must be found, which may take up a large part of the seller's time. That's why many companies invest in resources for these early stages so that their sales teams focus only on the subsequent more productive stages for them.

For example, in the contact identification and contact data phase it can be very useful to use the Linkedin network, which is ultimately the largest database of B2B prospects on the planet, and will help us to have a better idea of the company's activity and needs, to identify the appropriate contact, contact info, etc. At a minimum, we should see the company's website, review their corporate profile, news, networking activities, social profiles of contacts, etc.

This search process is not just by the seller or the company. The client also has their own search process, and such discovery should be a bidirectional process, so the phases of any sales process should be balanced with the way in which customers in our market buy and how they search for information.

The problem then is usually to align our sales process with the customer purchase process, which may also vary depending on the size of the target company.

Returning to the eternal paradigm of customer focus, we must place special emphasis on their interaction with the company in this process being considered as something of value, feeling that the time spent with us is useful, valuable, and persuading them to want to continue interacting with us in subsequent processes.

Having said that, we can list some of the sources of search for potential clients and methods of generating leads and prospects, which can be Inbound techniques (your clients come to you) or Outbound type (it is you who should find them):

- Cold calls and visits.
- References from other clients (referral selling).
- Traditional marketing and advertising (online and offline, social networks, specialized press, radio, TV, etc.).
- Email marketing.
- Content marketing.
- Co-branding/Co-marketing.
- Prospecting through social networks.
- Seminars/Presentations/Webinars/Podcasts.
- Social Selling.
- Networking.
- Databases and directories.
- Internet searches.
- Trade shows, conferences and exhibitions.
- Organisations and associations of the sector.
- Etc.

Each salesperson and company will need to define which one(s) are best suited to their type of business and market, especially considering the way in which their potential customers usually buy.

My advice to the curious reader is to inquire into each and every one of them (and others that are not listed, I repeat that this is not a bible), and not to discard any in advance.

Tip nº 42. Importance of Opportunity and Prospect Qualification

"There are some people who go through the forest and only see wood for the fire." (L. Tolstoi)

It's important for salespeople to focus their time and resources on opportunities that really are, on those that are most likely to develop.

That means being selective, it becomes necessary to qualify potential clients or prospects. Otherwise, you may have a big sales funnel full of "qualified leads", but you may be wasting time and effort addressing the wrong prospects with offers that can't be closed or that if they are closed, they just generate problems. It would be a clogged funnel.

It is necessary to qualify correctly and increase the conversion rates. Ideally, the seller should only work with genuine buyers.

A bad management of the prospect qualification process translates into a bad management of the entire sales process.

Note: we could also call it classification process, because that is what we do in essence by filtering and validating these contacts by giving them a rating and a quality level that meets our criteria, our own classification criteria for each prospect.

Actually in this stage of the sales cycle it is less about selling than about filtering, and it is better to look for the "No" than the "Yes" in practice. The salesperson should try to quickly discern which may be quality opportunities and which may not. Search and qualify quickly. In fact, this is one of the stages where most companies and sellers fail, in the whole prospecting phase in general, and particularly in the qualification phase.

It is necessary, on the part of the company and the salesperson, a motivation, mentality and positive attitude to improve this stage and understand the consequences it has on the final results, on the benefits and on selling more and better. Subsequent problems that can be found in negotiation or closing phases are most often determined by or caused by a poor initial qualification.

This qualification can be done in person, by telephone, by email, messaging, on-site or through automated means and programs, through social networks, etc. The ways can change, and we can combine all or several of them, but the need is there and it is of vital importance.

Thus, the prospect qualification is the process of determining whether a potential client is suitable and ready for our product or service.

Many companies and salespeople do not invest the time and effort required at this stage and in fact concentrate more on the massive generation of leads and prospects, so the advice is simple: analyze if you are correctly qualifying your prospects and if this can be the main cause of not selling more, because you are wasting a lot of time and money in chasing nonsense opportunities.

Tip nº 43. Prospect Qualification – BANT Method

"The journey of a thousand miles begins with one step." (Lao Tzu)

In one way or another, all sellers use a classification or qualification criteria, consciously or unconsciously. We seek to know if the customers have the need for our product, if they have money to buy and if that person is the one who decides or with the power to buy.

In the past, the acronym MAN was used for this, Money, Authority and Need, which in fact is still sufficient for most B2C transactions.

For the B2B area, it has been replaced by the BANT prospect qualification method: Budget, Authority, Need and Time, although some of the advice may also be applicable to B2C.

Basically, the concept of time has been added, since the purchase does not have to be made now even if the other three requirements are met. It was conceived a long time ago by IBM as a way to identify opportunities if the prospects met three of the four criteria.

For the curious reader, there are other methods, each one more or less adapted to the type of industry, such as ANUM (Authority, Need, Urgency and Money), FAINT (Funds, Authority, Interest, Need and Timing), CHAMP (Challenges, Authority, Money and Prioritization), MEDDIC (Metrics, Economic Buyer, Decision Criteria, Decision Process, Identify Pain and Champion), GPCT (Goals, Plans, Challenges and Timeline), NOTE (Need, Opportunity, Team and Effect), IFISU (Issue, Fit, Impact, Sponsor and Urgency), etc. But somehow the most widespread and well-known is the BANT on which we will focus.

Therefore, the seller must ask qualification questions to specify the following criteria that we will discuss:

- **Budget**: it is necessary to know the budget allocated for the purchase and that both parties assimilate if it is within the price range of our solutions. If we are in worlds far away in terms of what they intend to spend, it does not make sense to insist with who will not be able to pay or try to sell something outside of that budget. For example, in the case of car sales, it would be the case of trying to sell a luxury car to a customer who has a budget for a small car. Knowing the budget for the purchase helps the seller to define his offer. However, alternative forms of payment can always be sought or this economic situation may change in the future, so you have to be careful to discard the prospect by this criterion. On the other hand, if something excites us, we can say that we look for the money to get it.

It must also be said that in industrial sales this information is often not disclosed or the client does not want to express it quantitatively, but the seller must still try to find out whether or not there is a budget set aside or approved for the occasion, if there is a flexible financial plan, etc.

It is therefore convenient to find out: is there a budget? Is the budget for the project defined? Which budget best fits what you are looking for? Is it a negotiable budget? Is it yet to be approved? What does the approval depend on? Etc. It is normal that many potential clients do not want to share or reveal sensitive information, especially when they have only shown an initial interest and not a clear intention to buy, so these kinds of questions should be asked very carefully, sometimes indirectly, so as not to intimidate the prospect.

Sometimes it is not a matter of not having money, but that they are investing it in other initiatives or priorities, which will also have to be investigated. We must insist again that disqualification must not mean that you completely forget the prospect. They can change their situation and priorities in the future and it is always convenient to keeping them in our sights, educating and attracting them to our solutions. Ideally, we should be the ones to change those priorities.

Many times the budget is not approved or defined, but they begin to search in the market for possible solutions to the need. In that case you also need to find out what the budget approval process will be like and who is involved, who will have the authority to approve it.

Don't forget that many times more than finding out how big the budget is, the important thing is to find out how big the problem is.

- **Authority**: we need to know if the person we are dealing with has the final decision making authority, the authority to approve (or sign) the purchase or buy directly. If they don't have it, you need to find out who has it, or what group of people has it. Nowadays it is normal that the final decision is not made by just one person, but by a team, a buying group of several people (on average, up to more than five people) so it is necessary to involve all decision makers in the process. In this case, the main problem for the seller is usually to obtain the consensus of all parties.

Some of the answers we are looking for are: who makes the decision? How is the decision-making process? Are there different decision makers at different stages of the process? Is there a technical decision-maker other than the economic decision-maker?

Do we have access to those responsible for decision making? What is the buying process really like? How can all decision makers agree? Does the user or users of the product or service have something to say about it...?

On the other hand, the prospect may not have the power of decision but may be an "influencer", a recommender or specifier who can support our cause within the company or organization, recommending or specifying our product in other departments or to other higher instances. Therefore, we must never forget them, discredit them or lose our interest in them just because they don't have the absolute power to buy. In fact, in more complex industrial sales it is essential to have an internal employee ("champion" or "mobilizer" has been called by some) who really promotes change in that organization, who helps us determine who or whom to reach in the structure of the company and, above all, who helps us to influence them and put them in agreement. Moreover, the problem becomes more complicated when decision makers and mobilizers also differ from the end users of the product or service. It becomes even more complicated when there are intermediaries involved, for example contractors who are not the final buyer but who participate in the project in one way or another and are also part of the decision on suppliers.

It is also necessary to identify those who, for whatever reasons, are blocking or sabotaging the decisions rather than being decision-makers (yes, there are also someones like that!), and to find out why they are blocking or sabotaging them.

It is also common the existence of leads of specifiers or designers of specifications. For example, a design engineer, who may be studying the feasibility of a new application or product in which your product may have a place and who, although there is a current need, has no purchasing authority or budget and the time frame is indefinite. It would not meet the BANT criterion and nevertheless it is very important to help them, since they may introduce your product in future specifications, and without their recommendation we would never receive a real opportunity from that company. In fact, they are often involved in making lists of approved or authorized suppliers in which we should be. In this sense, the BANT criterion cannot be taken literally.

- **Need**: it is necessary to know if there is a need for our products or services, how they are currently solving the possible problems (also know if they are clients of our competition) and how important their needs are.

Some questions may include: how are they doing or solving it now? What problems do they encounter? What are the requirements? What are the consequences of not solving the problem or need? Why is it important within their plans or objectives? Are they common problems? Do they have a plan to solve it? What are the priorities? Are they willing to try other solutions? Are they open to change suppliers or expand suppliers? Can they benefit from our offer? What is the "pain" and how much can they handle it on a scale of 1 to 10? Why hasn't it been resolved before? How do they think the problem can be solved and why? What are their expectations? How can we help them meet their expectations? What problems do they expect to find to solve it? Etc.

We must confront their problems with our solutions, although we must remember that sometimes what a client or prospect say or express that needs is not really what they need and we must find out the real problem, the real need that they themselves do not know, whose consequences lead the client to a possible wrong conclusion of what they need (or to believe that they really do not need anything).

It is also important to find out whether they have bought something similar in the past and what problems they have encountered or on what basis they have made their purchase decision.

On the other hand, if they don't need any of our products or services it doesn't make sense to talk about other criteria (or is it? ... it's good to make the curious reader doubt a little...). We must also think that they may not need what you are offering them now, but they may need it in the future. They may not buy today, but they will buy tomorrow. Sometimes we also have to think about the long term, which will require our future following.

- **Time**: it is essential to know the time factor of the possible purchase, the time period, the decision making deadlines and when they may occur.

Some questions may include: in what period of time do they want the solution? What's their urgency? Which is the priority? Are other issues being resolved first? What is the time frame? Is this a realistic deadline? What problems can arise if the deadline is not met? In which part of the buying process are they? Have they just begun to evaluate alternatives? Etc.

When the matter is urgent, our speed of response and action will also be a decisive factor, so that we can convert it into an advantage for the purchase decision.

It is also interesting to find out which causes are delaying the decision and if you can influence them. The above three criteria may be met but may not be the right timing for the purchase or investment. Usually, the timeline of decision making also defines our criteria for following an opportunity, and that it be more or less "hot" or "cold", determining our priorities in this regard.

Thus, the BANT is a method of qualifying prospects used to identify and select the best prospects according to their budget, authority, needs and time frame.

You can also use a scale or score on each of the criteria to get a final score, but in the end the scoring or disqualification through that score is still subjective. The key is to understand whether they can represent real sales opportunities and to discern which ones have no chance. Therefore, each company should adapt this model according to their characteristics and type of potential customers in order to optimize it.

Having said that, it must be said that ... customers also lie (!). Yes, they lie (fortunately, not all of them), and sometimes they do so to overcome this qualification criterion, alleging for example a non-real budget and an equally false urgency, but ensuring our attention and help. So, not everything in the garden is rosy. Think about it.

It is necessary to find a balance between the desired number of potential clients and their quality, which is a matter of trial and error, and to continue testing. The qualification of prospects should always be an activity in test mode, independently of the fact that using CRMs and other marketing tools can automate the scoring and qualification criteria. There may also be a single non-negotiable criterion that quickly qualifies a prospect for being in or out and which does not require many additional steps.

Each market and type of product is a different world and it is the job of the seller and the company to adapt these criteria to each particular case.

Tip nº 44. Beyond BANT

"Intelligence is the ability to adapt to change" (Stephen Hawking)
"The only true wisdom is in knowing you know nothing." (Socrates)

Asking quality questions and practicing active listening is the key to correctly qualifying opportunities with the BANT criteria described. In any case, as commented in tip nº 14, the answers to the questions of the BANT criterion must have a specific, measurable and realistic nature, with clear objectives and framed within a period of time.

It is essential to know what objectives and plans the potential client has to satisfy their need, what problems they can find in that plan (and if our product can solve these problems) and what time frame they have for it, all of this with quantifiable and specific character. The more realistic and measurable the answers, the better we can advise and help the client. When their expectations are unrealistic, or they don't have a clear plan or goal, it is also an opportunity for the expert salesperson to guide them in this regard.

The qualification criteria aforementioned undoubtedly help to select quality leads, thus creating a better sales funnel. But in the current paradigm shift, where it is very important to educate and mature the prospects until they are ready to buy, as discussed in tip 39, the application of these criteria may leave out of our vision and action to potential clients who, even if they do not enter our sales funnel, should be attended, followed and not forgotten.

On the other hand, in today's customer-centric philosophy, we don't want just to sell to them, we want to help them identify, diagnose and solve their problem. The prospect expects the supplier to offer them value, to understand their problems and they do not want to be qualified or sold to, but we only give them value and confidence if they have money to spend today. They cannot trust us when we have decided that the potential client is not ready to buy and we lose interest in them. The day they're ready to buy, they won't call you, they'll buy someone else.

Many times it is not a question of needs or budget, but of priorities and consequences. Besides that, many decisions do not depend on a single authority, but on the decision process established in the company or by the client (which can also be changeable for each project). Understanding the client's situation, understanding their objectives and problems, their decision-making processes, their future plans, and understanding how our solutions can affect or help them can lead us to change their priorities, especially if we are able to show the impact that our solution can have on their business and the consequences of not doing so.

In that sense, even the time period of a possible purchase loses importance, what matters is when the client wants to have the competitive advantage that our product offers, the date when our solution effectively impacts on their objectives, and that is what will determine the purchase process. Convert the period or criterion from Time to Urgency.

If the client comes to understand, appreciate and desire the value we sell to them, then the budget appears and the priorities change.

Our value should be what guides their next steps to shorten the time frame of the agreement and move the opportunity forward. The same goes for the budget. The solution must be sufficiently beneficial for the customer to justify the purchase on the basis of the results they will obtain in return for the investment. There may not be a budget assigned at the beginning, but if there are sufficient reasons and priorities change, the purchase capacity and budget allocation end up happening.

Many businesses are not made due to the fear of making a mistake, for lack of confidence of the client to make the decision. It's easier to do nothing than take risks. They must be sure that they are making the right decision, and that this is better than what your competition may be offering. You must help the client to make an informed decision, help them in their purchasing process with our added value, demonstrate the ROI with data, trials, with our experience and competence, accompanying the client in each part of the process to help them to justify the purchase, from the time it is a prospect until after the purchase or installation of the solution, improving the customer experience also after the purchase, trying that they obtain the greatest possible benefit, increasing trust and promoting the word of mouth, thus turning these clients in loyal defenders of your brand, product or service.

From this point of view, the BANT is not enough, or at least it is not enough for all situations, contexts and prospects. We must go further, and as we have said above, it is about finding out objectives, plans, keys and challenges of the client that can help us to become not suppliers but partners of the client, helping them in their business.

As we said at the beginning, in the age of artificial intelligence, it is also a question of humanizing the experience. In the end, it's not just a matter of number of leads, but of the quality of the leads and prospects, and of improving that quality with our help. Each client is unique, different, and does not have to fit necessarily into our automated and programmed qualification criteria. We must go beyond the acronym, beyond the BANT.

It is no longer just a matter of selling advantages to a customer and overcoming their objections, but rather of helping a customer to identify the real problem and diagnose the impact of solving it, helping to make better decisions in the shortest possible time within a relationship of trust.

Besides that, we have already said that in today's complex environment most of the time the customers have advanced their purchasing process before we can determine what their need is, and they are probably already quite clear on how to solve the problem, so any attempt at qualification can be many steps behind their decision, and our ability to influence it can also be very small. In this sense, the qualification and positive perception of the client towards our capacity to help them is almost more important than our qualification to them, it is becoming more important the brand image and trust that we can generate as experts to be able to place ourselves at the beginning of their cycle of searching for solutions and not at the end, when one of our competitors may already be specified. In this regard, the work we can do with influencers and specifiers in our market or niche is becoming increasingly important.

Today's clients are looking for suppliers who understand their business and the problems they have to solve in their day to day. They are looking for solutions adapted to their particular case. We must demonstrate an understanding of these problems, offer ideas and solutions about their industry, and address any preconceived idea they may have about our product or service so that it is different and more trusted than our competitors.

Prospects can easily find information on prices, technical features and product comparisons on their own, but they need someone to give them a meaning and added value within their particular problem, their personal priorities and future plans. It is necessary that the salesperson adapts their sales process to each client to provide that additional value, a specific and different value for each client, aimed at collaborating in the customer's own success. And that also means going beyond the BANT.

Every time we connect with a potential client, with a sufficient degree of influence for the purchase decision (even if they are not the final "authority"), it is an opportunity to add value that has positive implications, demonstrating that we understand their problems, objectives and priorities in their particular industry. If we do this, selling will only be a consequence.

Since people like acronyms, if someone needs it, you can use this one, for example, to qualify your potential clients:

PISPOP: level of **Priority** and urgency, capacity for **Influence**, level of relevance that involves adopting a series of values and **Solutions**, wanting to solve a certain level of **Problems** or challenges and achieving quantifiable **Objectives** or beneficial effects with a specific and realistic **Plan** in which we can participate.

It's just a sympathetic idea, to be understood with a touch of humour, but it doesn't matter what acronym you want to invent, whether it's an acronym "friendly" for salespeople, easy to remember or not, the important thing is the change of mentality we've talked about in this tip. If your prospects are not moving forward in your funnel, maybe it's time to change your current approach. Instead of time, focus on priorities and urgency. Instead of authority, focus on the ability to influence. Instead of needs, focus on the problems and solutions and in the pursuit of profitable objectives that determine the budget allocation. You can and should use the BANT, but don't just stop there. Every client is a world of possibilities.

Tip nº 45. Initial Keys in the particular case of RFQ/RFP

"I'm not everything you see, but you don't see everything I am either." (Anonymous)

In the case of unknown leads, a previous research work is always necessary, especially regarding the origin of the lead. The salesperson's job is to find out as much information as possible about that lead/prospect or potential client, so that the call cold or contact is a little more "hot". The more we know about our client, the better.

It is interesting to comment the particular case of leads that generally come to us in the form of RFQ (Request for Quotation) or RFP (Request for Proposal) either by e-mail, by a filled contact form, by post or by any other means.

I am also referring to leads that have not been previously contacted and qualified. The receipt of a request for quotation/proposal may occur at a later stage in the funnel, as a result of the seller's previous work with the prospect. But this is not always the case, and what really interests us is to enter into the buying process of clients long before they are looking for different offers, so that they only consider ours from the beginning because they are convinced and persuaded of our advantages over other offers from competitors.

The "problem" is that the objective of an RFQ is mainly to compare prices from different offers, which is not what we want; we do not want to fight just for price. When the buyer launches an RFQ, it is assumed that they already know what they want and are inviting a number of suppliers to give them the best price and delivery time before selecting who will receive the order or job.

But for our interests, what is indispensable is to be the one specified, the one required, the one desired, and for this we have to enter and work with the client at an earlier time. The objective is that they only think about us and not the competitors. The objective is to avoid the generic RFQ or RFP, so that the client knows in advance that what they want is our option and they do not consider other alternatives. We can say that waiting until all requirements have been defined is often too late for our interests.

This is in line with what we have mentioned above of aligning our sales process with the client's purchase process. If we receive a request for a proposal from an unknown lead, and this is the first time we have heard of it and their need, there may already be a preferred alternative, and it may be difficult to change or influence their previous analysis of the market and the sought solution. But we have to try. And we must always think about the future and start to build trust with that prospect in our solutions so that the next time it is not necessary they launch a generic proposal, but that they have it clear from the beginning. Or if they launch it, that it be with our specifications.

We have already commented that this is not always the case, we will not always be able to start the process in an ideal way with the client from the beginning of the purchase process, and since this type of requests are very common, it is also necessary to give some hints about it.

As mentioned, the more we know about our potential client the better. Before contacting said lead, it is necessary to do the homework, and among other things, check and ask yourself the following questions:

1. **Check the origin of the RFQ/RFP:**
    - How the request came?
    - Who sent it? What company? Country? Do they have a website?
    - What is their position in said company? (Any social networks of the lead/s where we can find out more about them and their company?)
    - Are they a distributor? Are they an end customer? Intermediary?
    - Known or unknown? Do we have them in our database?
    - Are they from the competition? Is it of unknown origin?
    - Can we find out more? (e.g. through Google searches)
    - What is their job? Activity, context, situation? References (from other contacts already registered, social networks, etc.)? What needs may they have? What motivations? Etc.

2. **Check the object of the RFQ/RFP:**

   - Is it similar to previous requests? Will we have to offer the same to other leads?
   - Is this a recurring request? (Check previous offers and opportunities, their status, etc.)
   - Destination of the product/ service? Is it another country?
   - Is it a public tender? A project?
   - Is it a budgetary request?
   - Is it urgent? (Why?) Is there a deadline?
   - Is it just a request for information? (RFI)
   - Do we know if they have sent the same request to the competitors?
   - Are they asking for a competitor's product? (Is the name of the model mentioned or not?)
   - What are they really asking for? Are specifications or requirements attached? Are more specifications required? Can we offer alternatives or is it a closed request?
   - What special conditions are required? (identify elements such as transport, guarantees, payment methods, delivery date, validity of the offer, required discounts or any other requirement)
   - Do we really have anything to offer? Do we meet these specifications?
   - Is there any contradictory information?
   - Who should respond to this request? (Us or a distributor/representative?)
   - Is an urgent client visit required? Do they need a demonstration?
   - What next steps are required?

In short, when we receive such a request, we should not get nervous and immediately proceed to contact or sending an offer like crazy ... We must first verify the information we have and the information we can find out. We can continue with more steps later. But the first impression can be a mistake!

We must check if it can become a real opportunity, checking the origin, the purpose and reason of the request, in order to be able to act accordingly.

Checking and verifying all this information will help us to be better prepared for all the issues that may arise in the subsequent contact. In short, it is necessary to previously know as much as possible about our potential client and the request, especially when we are not the ones who have first contacted the prospect as a result of our search and market segmentation.

CHAPTER 8: ON THE SALES PROCESS

Tip nº 46. The Sales Process

"A knot can't be untied without knowing how it's done."
(Aristotle)

The sale is a process, and can have different stages, phases and subphases. Here we have already spoken about the first one, about the prospecting process, to which we have dedicated several tips to highlight its importance.

The sales process can be as complicated as we want; the important matter is to have a process, to have it clear and above all to apply it.

Simplifying, we could even reduce it to three steps: prospecting, developing (or managing opportunities) and closing business. Basically, convert a prospect into a client.

Each company and salesperson must define what their best process is and adapt it to their market, product or service, niche, etc.

We can expand it a little more and define more stages like this classic one:

- Prospecting.
- Needs detection.
- Argumentation.

- Proposal and Negotiation.
- Closing.

The more complex the sale, especially in B2B environments, the more we can define and expand the process that must be adapted to the specific needs of the sector. This is the process that we usually represent as a funnel and that should also be adapted as much as possible to the way in which our potential clients buy in that market or sector.

We can expand it even further and include some possible stages that will exist or not, and that will have more or less weight depending on the activity and the product. A slightly more complete process would be for example the following:

- Prospecting.
- Sales meeting/needs detection/Argumentation.
- Develop the solution.
- Presentation of the solution or product.
- Evaluation of the proposal/additional steps.
- Decision process/Negotiation.
- Closing.
- Supply/Implement solutions.
- Monitoring/measuring results.
- Loyalty building.

And we can also further define some sub-phases, some of which may or may not exist, or may overlap:

- Prospecting:
    - Definition of potential/ideal clients.
    - Searching for potential clients

- Qualification of prospects.
- Sales meeting:
    - Previous preparation.
    - Arrange a meeting.
    - Understand and validate the needs.
    - Diagnosis.
- Develop the solution:
    - Develop value proposal.
    - Develop economic offer.
- Presentation of the solution or product:
    - Previous preparation.
    - Argumentations.
    - Proposal
    - Economic offer.
- Evaluation of the proposal/additional steps.
    - Follow-up.
    - Demonstrations.
    - Other presentations.
    - Changes to the proposal.
    - Second and successive meetings.
    - New offers.
    - Other requirements.
- Decision process:
    - Objections.
    - Negotiation.
    - Agreements.
- Closing:
    - Closing.
    - Offer approval.
    - Contracts.

- Supply/Implement solutions:
    - Manufacturing.
    - Preparation of supply/installation.
    - Supply/installation.
    - Acceptance of supply/installation.
- Monitoring/measuring results.
    - After-sales assistance.
    - Corrections.
    - Measure results/feedback.
- Loyalty:
    - Client retention.
    - Loyalty building.
    - Get referrals / referral sales system.

Not all the sub-phases are always going to be there and not always in that order. Each one of the stages can be more or less long, they can overlap, they can happen in different order, some of them may need to be repeated, some of them can be mixed, etc. Of course, the payment process would also be included, but it can vary greatly in its position and time frame with respect to the other stages (payment in advance, after delivery, fractionated, 90 days payment, etc.)

The important thing is to define what the required or typical stages are in our market and from there to establish what are the milestones or events that must happen so that we can move from one to another and move forward the opportunity in our funnel. For example, one of the necessary milestones before moving forward could be the product demonstration, which must be planned and scheduled with the client and being executed.

There will be cases where the sale can be closed during a first presentation and others where several additional steps are required. The important thing is to always establish with the client at each step a series of agreements that lead us to the next step. Each event or phase must be directed for the final close, so this stage can occur in any of them. The argumentation and handling of objections can also take place throughout the entire process, as well as the realization of various proposals.

If we do not get the final agreement or closing in any of the stages, it is always necessary to make it clear with the client what the next step is, and to obtain from the client "micro-agreements" where both parties could have clear the commitments, actions by both parties and the dates established for the following phases, always thinking of advancing the sales opportunity throughout the phases and sub-phases mentioned. Of course, in each and every one of the phases we must not forget to add value and to apply each and every one of the advice we have mentioned so far.

The important thing is to have an established process, which does not have to be just in the salesperson's mind, a process that we can control, measure, repeat, make predictable and that we can manage and optimize. Only companies that have their sales process defined can improve it. There may be opportunities that stop at one part of the process or the other, for whatever reasons that we will have to analyze, but if we do not systematize the process we cannot analyze it or improve it.

And you, reader ... Do you have a defined sales process? If you don't have any, you can start designing one now... and follow it.

Tip nº 47. The Previous Preparation

"Luck is what happens when preparation meets opportunity."
(Seneca)

In general, every opportunity we have to meet with a client should be minimally prepared, and this means being clear on the important and essential points that must be addressed, and which should not be forgotten.

It is very important to work previously such meeting, visit, trade show, conference via internet, visit of clients to your company, etc. The previous preparation is one of those phases to which the salesperson does not usually spend much time, but which is precisely essential for the success of the process and for the subsequent steps to be followed throughout the sales process we have mentioned, so it is important to highlight it as advice.

You have to improvise as little as possible.

The key to the success of the sale often lies in the previous preparation, and this also includes trying to get to know the client in advance, if possible, to get information about them, the company, to know their possible needs, their possible problems, and to compare them with our possible solutions. If we have already qualified them previously, by telephone or other means, we may know some things about them, but before any personal meeting or any additional contact, it is always necessary to go further, go deeper into our preparation.

If possible, we must first look for information about your client, their company and their previous contacts with your company, the previous opportunities, why they bought or why they stopped buying, their needs, previous motivations, their market and activity, etc. Do a thorough investigation of what your client wants and the reasons why they need it.

In many cases the problem is not to know the client of your client. If your product is going to solve problems of the final client of your client, it is essential to know what these problems are and how your product can be the solution, so we will have to investigate previously in this regard.

The previous preparation also includes having ready and on hand a whole series of sales tools that can help us. This includes, among many other things: catalogues (which should be updated), price lists, offers, cards, promotional gifts, press articles, comparisons with the competition, technical notes, presentations (adapted to the specific needs of the customer or audience), videos, etc. And if possible, also the product itself, if it is necessary to demonstrate it, if the client needs to touch it, use it, try it, or simply see it physically.

We must also use the advantages that technology gives us today, and if for example it is necessary to make videos of use or installation of the product, or how to solve a problem that will help the sale or service of the product, then let's not stop doing it and have it ready.

Another of the essential sales tools are the lists of satisfied customers, the references, the recommendations, which are also very powerful tools that we can and should use. Of course, do not stop using technology in its many facets and contributions, laptop, tablet, mobile, etc., that are also sales tools.

In short, when you are going to talk to a client, you MUST be prepared.

As per the initial sentence, you make your own luck. Are you ready to be lucky?

Tip nº 48. Development of the Proposal

"Plans are only good intentions unless they immediately degenerate into hard work." (Peter Drucker)

Once we have understood and validated the client's needs, problems, goals, objectives, the plans for developing possible solutions and the implications of not doing them, along with the deadlines for implementing them, we need to develop our proposal, if we have not already done so in the same meeting and diagnosis phase.

Here it is also convenient to remember the previous steps specified in tip nº. 45 when it is the particular case of an RFQ/RFP, which are also applicable.

The development of our proposal may involve a series of steps and advice to be followed, which again, do not all have to be necessary or in this order, which will depend on the activity, product and market, but that should also systematize and adapt to our particular case to have more chances of success, such as the following ones:

- **Identify and confirm all documentation regarding needs and/or requirements**: the compliance with the mandatory requirements is essential. This may be the case, for example, if there are a series of technical specifications of the product or service, studies, administrative requirements, authorizations, legal requirements, obligatory conditions, etc. It is very important to be clear about everything we have to comply with and not forget or ignore any requirement. Anything that we do not comply with may be the reason for our proposal to be rejected. If there are unclear or confusing requirements that could lead to errors, they need to be clarified with the client. Remember that we must fully understand the real client's needs.

- **Respond within the stipulated period:** if we have committed ourselves to the client within a given time frame, we must comply with it. Otherwise it's one of the easiest ways to discard about proposal in comparison with that of the competition. If the proposal depends on a team of several people and/or departments, they must be coordinated and committed to deadlines. Someone may be needed to lead and distribute the tasks.

- **Define our specific strategy:** basically decide what fits best in our proposal to the client. This may include, among others:
    - To analyze all our possible solutions that meet the needs and problems of the client (and that meet the defined specifications or requirements) and to study which ones can have more options of success, and especially if there is a better option, viable, that can exceed the expectations of the client. Can we go further with additional values? Can we differentiate ourselves with benefits and advantages that go beyond what is expected? How can we make our solution more beneficial to the client's goals and

plans? It's also about creating the "wow" effect in the client.
- Analyze the alternatives of the competitors and the possible proposals/offers/prices of said competition.
- If the needs/specifications are not met, we must analyze our best possible option (if justified).
- To study if it is necessary to offer alternative options or different proposals to the main one, accessories, complementary products, etc.

- **Define our economic strategy**: once all the above has been clarified, it is convenient to study how our proposal is going to be implemented in economic terms, and this may include, among other considerations:
    - Is there a target price relative to an allocated budget?
    - Is there any type of discount? (And study the conditions for this. Discounts must be justified in any case)
    - Are there commissions for intermediaries, distributors, representatives, agents, etc.?
    - Should our proposal be based or considering previous prices to the same client?
    - Is it a closed price for a package? Is it based on quantities?
    - Are we the specified/desired one and this situation needs a specific strategy?
    - Do we rely on prices from competitors we know or can we get to know?
    - Is a second round expected?

- Will we offer several options? How do we differentiate them and highlight the main one or the one we want?
- Will we offer several clients the same thing? Same economic proposal or will it vary?
- Required terms: payment methods, transport included or not, delivery time (does it fit the required one?), training conditions if necessary, installation or supply conditions, validity of the offer/proposal, urgency required? Guarantees? etc.

- **Prepare the relevant documentation:**
    - Substantiate the proposal in writing taking into account all the above. An important advice in any case is always to personalize the proposal, to adapt it to the specific client (and not to abuse the cut-paste! or at least try it's not noticed...) Of course, we must take into account all the points defined in our previous strategy, developing the advantages and benefits, what the client will get and what it will make for them. Justify the options and conditions.
    - Substantiate the additional evidence or documentation that supports the proposal. Many times it is necessary to prove our advantages and benefits with facts, performance tests, audits, authorizations, type cases of other clients, references, surveys, studies, technical documentation, plans, etc. Sometimes the need for specific documentation that increases the value of our

proposal may arise during the development of the proposal.

- **To define the presentation of the proposal**: to define the means and modes of presentation that can be very varied depending on the product, sector and activity. It can be in person, by email, letter, through intermediaries, meetings with interested parties, etc. In any case, the best option is always to review the proposal WITH the client, in a scheduled meeting.

- **Review of the whole proposal**: it is always convenient to review all the work, a final check that can also incorporate last minute needs or requirements. Final changes, checks, any additional value for the same money? Any way to add more value? Is it really beneficial for the client? Additional tasks? Are we using all our sales tools within our reach? Is there a final call to action? Is it realistic? Are defined the following actions and steps? Did we miss anything?

In any case, we must always try to make our proposal/offer simple, eliminate barriers to the client, insist on each and every one of the tips we have mentioned and not forget to seek excellence, build trust, use clear language, focus on customer needs, build relationships and provide the best customer experience at all times.

And two final pieces of advice:

Any process is better than no process at all.

Apply the lessons learned from the previous ones to the following processes and improve them gradually.

Tip nº 49. On the Objections

"The brave man is not he who does not feel afraid, but he who conquers that fear." (Nelson Mandela)

We have already said that objections can arise at any point of the sales process, at any stage, and that they should somehow be understood as opportunities rather than problems. We have also discussed the cause of many of them in the part of the price objection, which is usually one of the main ones, and we have also spoken there of some ways of dealing with them, which can be extrapolated to any other objection.

There is a lot of information on the subject and a lot of techniques for dealing with objections that the curious reader can investigate if he or she is interested, although it is important not to trust just in prefabricated sentences, nor with the series of response-counter response types, which may be useful at any given time, but which are not applicable to all sectors, products, cases, people and situations.

What I want to emphasize here is mainly the importance of the previous preparation. You have to do your homework. In each market, in each type of product or service, in each type of industry or sector, there are usually a series of typical objections (sometimes only a dozen), which can be related to the product, the service, its usefulness, advantages and disadvantages, competition, misunderstandings, preconceived ideas or personal motivations of security, trust or distrust, pride, interest, comfort, etc.

The salesperson must detect and collect this series of typical objections of their sector and products, and work on them, create an sales pitch that must start with an in-depth knowledge of product, your own company, your competition, the market and your own strengths and weaknesses.

You have to establish the critical points of your product that will generate objections, and ask yourself, for example:

- Why should they use our product?
- What benefits will the customer get?
- What are the advantages and disadvantages?
- What are the typical barriers and problems?
- What are the most common psychological barriers to such a product or service?
- What advantages can overcome the disadvantages?
- What are the typical objections related to comparisons with the competition, both in price and in other aspects?
- What objections can be converted into purchase reasons?
- What are the typical negative aspects to be neutralized and guided?
- What objections should be prevented and anticipated?
- Which are trivial and which increase the resistance of the buyer?
- Which ones need demonstrable evidence to fight the lack of trust?
- What are generally false or misleading in my sector?

All critical points and typical objections that may arise must be worked out previously, establishing the best answer, solution and way to overcome the objection.

50. Keys to Remember in Any Negotiation

"An eye for an eye only ends up making the whole world blind."
(Mahatma Gandhi)

Many negotiations become pure bargaining, and that is not those that I am referring to, because if it is reached that point it is because we have not previously defended our value proposal or we have not made any and there is no value to defend beyond price. But many times throughout the purchasing process (not always in the end) there is a need to negotiate terms and conditions and characteristics of the business relationship in order to reach agreements that are satisfactory to all parties (sometimes they are more than only two parts). Basically we can say that: negotiation = solution of a problem.

We must remember that any negotiation is also an opportunity to improve the relationship with our clients and that it should not be understood as a confrontation, which does not mean that positions and competing interests cannot be maintained, which will have to be solved without affecting relations, seeking solutions that pursue a level of results and satisfaction of both parties, a win-win situation.

So, it is convenient to give some typical keys, although I repeat that this is not a bible nor does it pretend to be one, so the curious reader can go deeper into the many treatises, books and courses on the subject, and here we just give a few hints and advice as the following:

- The important thing is always the business to negotiate, and the problems belong to the course of the negotiation, it is not

necessary to take it personally. You have to separate people from problems (hard on problems, soft on people)
- Always remember the needs of the parties and seek the best solution for both. Everybody can win.
- All proposals are valid in advance; they should not be disqualified without having studied them. It is about discovering and exploring options and criteria. Points of conflict are resolved by looking for options, different ways to satisfy the interests of the parties, as well as highlighting points on which there may be agreement.
- Try to find and understand the interests behind the positions. If we do not discover the interests, we will not be able to find solutions. Interests that can be shared, opposed or different. One thing is what people say they want and another thing is what they really want or motivate them to stay in a position and make a decision.
- If the other loses, it doesn't always mean that I win. All interests are not opposed. It is a question of reaching satisfactory agreements but with objective and achievable criteria.
- Different interests can complement each other even if they have nothing to do with each other now; it is a question of how to make them compatible.
- Always evaluate the possibility of increasing the cake, which can be convenient for both parties if there are shared interests.
- Interests should not be taken for granted, they should be discovered. For example, a buyer may place a strict condition that the product be delivered within a week, but this may be due, among other things, to a hidden interest in changing

suppliers, or to waiting for new customers and having an unexpected increase in consumption.
- We must dialogue, not preach or impose. And communication must be bilateral and efficient. If you hold inflexible positions is not a negotiation but an imposition. That doesn't mean that pressure elements cannot be used as long as they do not threaten the confidence and become a duel of egos.
- It is necessary to put oneself in the place of others (empathy), not to blame others for the problem (not to generate defense mechanisms), to help them get involved (how could we solve this?) and to recognize and understand the emotions that arise. Remove tension and allow the other party to vent, without giving concessions for emotional explosions. We all have the right to make mistakes and to rectify them. And if it's appropriate, you should also apologize if the circumstances require it.
- We must not give in to the pressure, only to reason and to objective and independent criteria, which must be sought.
- Cultural differences must always be considered. This implies not assuming that they understand us in everything (they can understand something different), there can be problems of perception and different beliefs.
- Actively listen and consider both verbal and nonverbal cues. Ask questions that counteract rigid positions, avoiding frontal attacks. Ask questions about the context, the problem, the consequences and the results. We have interest in why? And why not? How to deal with the problem? What is the way of doing business with them? We are interested in the client's point of view and how to work with them.

- When generating options it is good to practice creativity (brainstorming) to complement different interests.
- There's no need to be in a hurry.
- The agreement must be fair.
- Commitments and agreements must always be clear, as well as a plan for their implementation.
- It is always advisable to have a BATNA, a "best alternative to a negotiated agreement", an alternative plan prepared in advance if no agreement is reached that satisfies your interests, which is non-negotiable and should be a good alternative when all of the above fails. We also need to think about what the BATNA of the other party might be.
- The offers to present (it is convenient to have more than one) must be modifiable, upgradeable, and not closed positions, and must include specific factors of the interests of the other party that we have discovered, clearly indicating the (realistic) benefits that will be obtained by accepting our offer. The possible counteroffer must also be prevented.
- As always, it is important to stress the importance of the previous preparation to the negotiation, and of preparing the whole strategy that will have to be in line with discovering the interests, separating the people from the problems, generating options with objective criteria and having offers that can reach mutual agreement or in the worst case to the BATNA. It's about minimizing improvisation.

There is nothing new in all this and it is based on logic, on common sense, and on thinking that agreements will make your job as a salesperson much easier and will contribute to your business success. People are the ones who make a company work or fail. And the negotiation is between people...

Tip nº 51. Considerations on the Closing

"... If you can talk with crowds and keep your virtue,
Or walk with Kings—nor lose the common touch,
If neither foes nor loving friends can hurt you,
If all men count with you, but none too much;
If you can fill the unforgiving minute
With sixty seconds' worth of distance run,
Yours is the Earth and everything that's in it,
And—which is more—you'll be a Man, my son!"
(Rudyard Kipling)

If at this stage of the book you still think you're going to find a series of magic phrases here to force a closing of the sale, you are one of those who still thinks that closing is the most important part of selling and that you have to close to the minimum opportunity ... if so: you're punished! ... Read all the tips again from the beginning, but this time carefully ... and if possible twice...

Jokes aside, we have said that selling is a process; it has a series of steps and previous preparations, aimed not only at closing, although also, but above all to customer satisfaction and to exceed their expectations, to get their loyalty and commitment. It's not a matter of closing a deal today, but that they buy us again and it's all about building customer loyalty.

In this whole process and with the mentality of selling without selling as we said in that tip, if we have done it well, the closing is a stage that takes place as a natural consequence of the above and that is not necessary to force with any trick.

The closing is a result, it is not a cause of the sale, but a consequence of having sold well.

Of course we have to ask for the close, let's not go crazy and forget about closing the deal. We must not be afraid of closing either, nor to do it in a weak, shy way, as if we were begging to be bought. You have to look for and ask for the commitment of the client and propose an action plan that can be either to accept a quote, to sign or confirm an order, to make a contract, or other commitment (if and only if they have the authority to do so).

You have to close with conviction, without being aggressive, but with the certainty that the client has accepted all the advantages and benefits that we offer, that they want to solve their problems and needs and that there is not any problem or objection left to solve that will make them regret or not buy again. In short, when we are sure that they are convinced, persuaded and seduced by our proposal.

Of course, it's not about selling at any cost, or selling by force. If we sell and then the buyer doesn't get the profit they expected, if they don't get the value they expected, we will have created a dissatisfied customer. And that's not our goal.

As in the domino game, the close is just other piece, and all the pieces must be perfectly aligned and in the right direction to produce the domino effect, so that the whole sales process is successful. Close is not the last step, nor the last piece. The priority element is the search for customer satisfaction and loyalty. It is not about closing an operation today, but about customer loyalty and the purchase repetition. The recommendation to third parties will follow the domino effect.

The search for customer satisfaction and loyalty are priority elements or they are not. There's no middle ground. The most successful companies and sellers are those that consistently satisfy their customers and manage to retain them. Period. We invite the curious reader to read again the tip no. 46 on the sales process, and to note that the last step of the process is not the closing but the customer loyalty. It's not even the penultimate...

Returning to the subject of closing, what is also a big mistake is to try to close prematurely, when the argument has been scarce, when the client has not considered or accepted any benefit for them, when the perceived costs are greater than these benefits and when we have not generated enough value and purchase reasons.

It must also be said that not all closings necessarily involve a sale. They can be small commitments from the client or prospect that we want to get to make advance the opportunity, they can be micro-closures or milestones within our sales process to, for example, get the commitment of a demonstration or want to try the product, get access to the final decision maker with the support of the influencer, get technical approval of our product in a department, get a supplier approval, get the acceptation of a partial action plan of a project, etc.

In this sense, the final closing can be understood as the last of a series of micro-closures and commitments that we have been agreeing with the client throughout the sales process and that lead us to finally close the opportunity in a satisfactory way for both parties.

In short, we will close more, we will close better and the closing will be a natural consequence if...:

- If we have taken into account the principles and eternal advice to treat our customers.
- If we have made all the habits of the excellent salesperson our own.
- If we have adapted our value proposition to each client and have helped them to buy.
- If we have generated the necessary trust in the client.
- If we have been creative and have applied with balance the art of relationship with the science of selling.
- If we have found out the basis of our sale and what needs we can satisfy.
- If we have discovered the needs of our clients and we have motivated and stimulated them.
- If we have helped to buy, to solve problems, with passion, without manipulating or forcing the sale.
- If we have addressed the heart and mind of the client, with arguments and emotions that convince and persuade them, and if we have looked at our business and product through their eyes.
- If we have put the focus on the client and have not made any of the typical mistakes of the salespeople.
- If we know well what we are selling, our product, our market and our customers, putting ourselves in their shoes with empathy and we have used all the necessary skills of the salesperson.

- If we have not become robot-sellers and have changed our perspective of future and specialization to be mainly consultants rather than order takers.
- If we have been able to listen to our client and have found out their real problems.
- If we have practiced active listening to better understand our client.
- If we have asked intelligent questions to get quality answers that will allow us to help them.
- If we have got specific, measurable and realistic answers to their problems, plans and objectives.
- If we have been proactive and have discovered why they buy from us and why they don't buy from our competitors.
- If we have avoided having arguments with the client with a service attitude, interest in building the relationship and solving problems.
- If we have understood and used the messages beyond verbal communication.
- If we have avoided competing only for price and know our competition well.
- If we have applied some of the keys to differentiate ourselves from our competitors and have positioned ourselves in the client's mind in a differential way.
- If we have sold our difference and given the customer reasons to buy.
- If we have been able to communicate well our memorable unique selling proposition.
- If we have sold benefits and competitive advantages that meet the particular needs of the client.

- If we have provided excellent customer service throughout the entire sales process.
- If we have generated value and increased the perceived value, making the client perceive and value properly all the whole set of benefits, including all the subjective and emotional concepts and advantages that weaken the price.
- If we have cleared the smoke screen behind the price objection, turning it into additional opportunities, and above all if we have prevented them from happening.
- If we have reduced or eliminated the negative costs in your client's mind, such as time, psychological and effort and energy costs.
- If we have considered optimizing the customer experience in each and every one of the interactions with them, increasing our value and the degree of customer satisfaction.
- If we have built a bond of trust from the beginning with our prospect, improving their experience.
- If we have used all the tools at our disposal to improve that experience in order to get their loyalty, the repeat purchase and their recommendation to third parties.
- If we have correctly identified our ideal client and have taken into account all the phases of the prospection.
- If we have defined the sources of search for potential customers that best suit our business.
- If we have correctly qualified our potential client with the criteria most appropriate to our objectives and theirs.
- If we have aligned our sales process and solutions with our customers' purchasing process to provide that additional value in line with their problems, plans, projects and objectives.

- If we have managed to be the ones specified without waiting for generic purchase requests.
- If we have defined a sales process that we can control, measure, repeat, make predictable and that we can manage and optimize.
- If we have made our own luck with all the necessary previous preparation with any client.
- If we have correctly developed our proposal, in a systematic and complete way, focused on the needs and problems of the client.
- If we have worked our sales speech, not only to neutralize any objections that may arise, but also to avoid them.
- If we have taken into account all the keys to negotiating correctly, without improvisation, in line with the interests, separating people from problems, and have generated options and offers with objective criteria to reach a satisfactory agreement for all parties.
- If we have sought and requested the client's commitment to a plan of action throughout a series of agreements...

... In short: if we have followed the advice given in this book, then the closing will be a logical consequence of all that.

Are you still worried about how to close well? Or are you still not sure why you don't sell more and have more success selling? ... If so, you have to repeat the treatment for your disease of bad sales ... I advise you to go back to the beginning.

CHAPTER 9: THE VISIT OF CR

"Success is dependent on effort." (Sophocles)

Without noticing it, we have reached the end of this book ... Some advice has been left in the pipeline, as there were quite a few topics to be discussed. But the goal was to reach 51, although in reality there are many more as the reader will have observed, until reaching hundreds among all that has been said in each one of them. I hope in any case that it has helped you, motivated and inspired you for your work, business and profession...

"... I was really inspired by it..."

"Ahhhhh! ... Again I hear voices! ... Who are you? Are you Jin...?"

For those who don't know, Jin is very funny Samurai spirit that starred the Smab book story, and who appeared from time to time.

"No, I'm not Jin, but I couldn't miss this opportunity."

"Who are you then....? You scared me.... the thing is that I hear you in my head like as it happened with Jin but you don't have his characteristic cherry blossom smell..."

"I'm the Curious Reader, CR for friends."

How? ... It can't be ... How are you here? I mean, you should be above the paper or in front of the screen, I don't know... You should be reading!"

"Well, like I said, I couldn't miss it. Besides that, you have quoted me more than twenty times in this book and about ten times in the previous one. You've mentioned the curious reader many times, and ... that's me! It was now or never and I wanted to give you my opinion and ask you some questions."

"I find it strange, CR ... can I call you that, right? ... But well, I don't always have the opportunity to talk to a reader inside a book, and less with one as curious as you. You're not a spirit, are you…?"

"No, I'm not. I'm flesh and blood, but somehow I managed to get into your book. I've been following you since the last one and I wanted to thank you for inspiring me and helping me with your advice. They are coming in handy in my profession, I have learned new facets in the world of sales, refreshed concepts that are sometimes forgotten and I have understood the reason for many common practices. It will be very profitable for me and will help me to sell more and succeed selling."

"I'm so glad, CR. As I said at the beginning, if you have found even just one valuable advice for you, I will have fulfilled my goal. Thank you very much."

"Moreover, as I am curious, you have encouraged me to seek and deepen my knowledge on many topics which, as you say, each one is a world. It is true that today it is essential that we train ourselves continuously."

"Sure, CR. That's why I mentioned you, to encourage you to do it. On the other hand, imagination, curiosity and the spirit of discovery move the world today more than knowledge. As Albert Einstein said, 'I have no special talent. I am only passionately curious.'"

"Thanks for the quote. By the way, I also really liked the quotes you have added in each tip. They have made me think."

"That was also what it was about."

"But tell me, I'm just curious, of course ... Why 51 tips exactly?"

"Ah! ... Okay, I'll explain: it's related to the famous number 101 that usually appears in many publications of all kinds, and that alludes to the basic knowledge of a subject. 101 means an introduction or overview of a knowledge, and is intended to imply that some additional information is given beyond others that include only 100 topics of a subject. I wanted these tips to be not just an overview or a basic knowledge, but to contribute something else, a few more steps or one more level. So, according to the emblematic phrase "less is more", I'm left with half a hundred plus one, wanting to contribute that additional something also with the 51, instead of just 50."

"And isn't it because 101 was going to be too long and extensive?"

"Shut up! ... shhh ... now that no one can hear us ... at first I thought of 101, but then I realized that so many tips required an additional extension and I preferred the option that I mentioned."

"It is understood. I don't know, but it seems to me that someday you'll reach 100 ... Changing the subject, and why isn't this book like the previous one, with a story and characters, why isn't it a storytelling? I expected a similar style."

"Thanks for asking, CR. But now you're giving it a touch of story too! ... I'll tell you: after a presentation, people remember 5% of what they've been told, while if they're told a story they remember more than 60%. In that case it was necessary to tell it so that the eternal concepts would be engraved in the memory and also to make it more enjoyable and easy to read. In this case, the 51 tips are intended to be reread over and over again, so that you can make them yours and apply them. It's about reading and rereading each piece of advice as if you were climbing a ladder, step by step. And climb it as many times as necessary. No story is going to replace that necessary effort. In this regard, read again the opening sentence of Sophocles of this chapter ... In any case, these are the tips I would have liked to have received when I started selling 20 years ago. I would have taken them into account and I'm sure I wouldn't have had so many mistakes. I hope you'll do the same."

"I will keep them in mind, reread them, and I will make them my own. Thank you very much for this last advice, which has to do with the effort. By the way, will there be more? Will there be a third volume of the series?"

"Well, that depends on you ... It depends on how much you liked it and if you are a satisfied reader. Curious but happy. And it depends on that you may recommend it. You're the one who can contribute to the continuation of the series with its success."

"Well, that's what I'll do, because I would like more. By the way, how did you get inspired in this book?"

"The truth, CR, is that the muses visit you when they want to, not when you want ... but one of the main inspirations has been to see that the first book has been very well received by readers and that it is helping many people, which has encouraged me to continue writing. With this second book my goal is the same, to help all professionals, and you too, with this series of tips and ideas that help to complete the vision of this complex world of sales, making it more understandable and manageable."

"Great. Any final advice?"

"Believe in yourself, CR. And may you be happy."

"Surely yes, and I'll follow your advice. Thank you very much and see you."

"Thanks to you, CR. And I hope to see you soon. A big hug, which I hope may pass through the paper or the screen, just like you have done…"

THE END

Author's Note

Thank you for coming all this way, thank you for being there. I hope to see you again soon.

If you liked the book, I would like to ask you, **please make a brief and positive review** of it in the online bookstore where you bought it. It just takes a minute.

And if you have enjoyed more than you expected, if it has made you think, if you have learned or re-learned, and if this book has helped you, please make others happy and recommend it to your friends, family, contacts and colleagues. They'll thank you too, and that's what it's all about. Thank you. A thousand thanks.

Author page: http://www.amazon.com/author/raulgilo

Twitter: https://twitter.com/RaulGilo

Linkedin: https://www.linkedin.com/in/raulsanchezgilo

Email: raulvendermasymejor@gmail.com

Printed in Great Britain
by Amazon